THE WINTERS OF MY SUMMER AFTERNOONS

Eric Le Roy

Silent E Publishing Company

Copyright © 2021 Eric Le Roy
and Silent E Publishing Company

Silent E Publishing Company
4446 Hendricks Ave, #141
Jacksonville, FL 32207

ISBN-13: 978-1-941091-17-3

1 2 3 4 5 6 7 8 9

CONTENTS

Section 1: Backroads to the Green Palace

1. Mandarin and That Cavender Boy   9
2. O, Vapid Voyeur, Let's Walk in the Rain 19
3. Phantom Friends and Night Music   29
4. Not to Waste Your Life   39
5. Megapolis   45
6. A Catcher in the Rye   51

Section 2: Say-Hey Days

7. Canned Laughter   57
8. The Sleek Bleak Utterness of Make-Believe 63
9. The Iron Necklace of Ordinariness   77
10. How Much Hair Do You Want in Your Soup? 87
11. My New York City Blues   97
12. All-Night Diners and Eternal Darkness 105
13. The Graceful Vertigo of the Sky Noodles 111
14. The Dawns and Twilights of Offices   121
15. The Enchanted Recycling of Old Mothers 129
16. The Silence and the Darkness   147
17. That Raspberry Face   155

Section 3: The Summers of My Winter Afternoons

18. The Valley of the Shadow of Death   165
19. Death is No Laughing Matter Except Sometimes 175
20. Wings of My City   181
21. Benedetta   189
22. When I Was Judas   199
23. The Narrow Path to the Far North   215
24. Forgiveness Sunday   221
25. Thoughts That Dominate   229
26. Farewell to the Village   235

4

INTRODUCTION

The Writing life

I met Eric Le Roy when we were both students in the writing program at the University of Florida in 1980. That was a long time ago, but in that odd way that our memories have of reopening certain sealed tunnels (or tombs, in some cases), to me, he is still that bushy-haired young man with the alert eyes, the generous laugh, and that love for words that shone forth in both his conversation and his writing. Naturally, it was a time for naive ambitions, and cheap but hefty beers in the Sportsman's Lounge or the Windjammer in Gainesville, all-night discussions that were alternately charming and tawdry and filled with the wild aspirations of young people who believed in what they were up to.

How strange then, that after more than forty years, even though I now see him once in a while through the time-warping window we call video chat, that is the Eric I think of. Oh, he is still wide-eyed, still an excellent conversationalist, still gulping down life with every breath, it seems, and still a hell of a lot of fun to talk with. Yet... the truth that we are both merely a short shuffle away from being two old men rehashing tales from their prime, such as it was, hangs in the cyber air. Like me, he has the gift-curse of a finely sharpened recall for details; there is no story from those days that I can begin without his being able to finish it or tell it better.

Of course, it is not as if the years that have trundled hastily away have been without their varied cargo. Eric has lived in more places around this creaking globe than most of us have even imagined, and I know that his life has been as full as that of anyone I've known, full of the loves and sorrows and longings and successes that some of us will experience if we hang around long enough. I know this because a number of them are accounted in this very book. I have struggled to find a word for these pieces of writing; the traditional term is "essays," I suppose, but I would argue that they are more like musings or meditations, and still they roam far from esoteric philosophizing. They are the observations of the common man, if the common man had the eye and voice of a poet.

In the end, the reward of the writing life is not in fame and fortune. Those are graven images. The artist cannot avoid living in a particular way: he regards the world with both the keen, cold vision of the explorer always approaching the undiscovered land and with all of the self-consuming desire of a starved lover. Certainly, it is the sort of life that can cause pain, but its myriad joys are there for the taking as well. Whoever you are that has picked up this volume, I urge you to spend some time in the world of Eric Le Roy. It is a big place, but you will find that it is one that you, too, know very well.

Jeff Trippe
June 2021

1.

BACKROADS TO THE GREEN PALACE

MANDARIN AND THAT CAVENDER BOY

But this morning the shoe-box house on the back porch is empty.
Where has he gone, my meadow mouse,
My thumb of a child that nuzzled in my palm? —
To run under the hawk's wing,
Under the eye of the great owl watching from the elm-tree,
To live by courtesy of the shrike, the snake, the tom-cat.
I think of the nestling fallen into the deep grass,
The turtle gasping in the dusty rubble of the highway,
The paralytic stunned in the tub, and the water rising, —
All things innocent, hapless, forsaken.

© FROM "THE MEADOW MOUSE" BY THEODORE ROETHKE

Our latest cat has disappeared. My wife and I call him Mandarin. Or Tangerine. Because of his color of course, though it is really more tawny than bright orange. We live in Bulgaria with two Moscow dogs and an old cat from Siberia named Thomas. Mandarin is a feral cat, born locally.

Out here in this village there are many feral cats, and like feral cats everywhere (including human ones) they come and go without anyone taking much notice. When our dogs are off the leash during walks in the valley (I keep them close on our dusty little street at the edge of the deepening glade and then turn them loose to gallivant in the fields), they will chase any cat they see. They never catch them and wouldn't know what to do if they did. They are not pit bulls or Rottweilers; besides, the quicksilver, wily cats always manage to get up a tree, over a fence, or under a gate.

But the dogs are never discouraged. It's the same with their attitude to rabbits and birds and lizards. Their optimism in beginning the chase never relents; their inevitable failures never chagrin nor humble them. Only with snakes have I had to intervene.

But everybody knows, regardless of what you see on YouTube, that dogs and cats have an uneasy relationship.

That's what made it all the more amazing when one twilit evening a couple of months ago (warm weather having come at last), the slightly built but streamlined little Mandarin simply walked out of the shadows as we all sat on the patio, strolled up to the large dogs and lay down like a feather between them. No fear. He simply rolled over on his back and stretched elegantly out like a prince having a picnic outside the Taj Mahal.

The dogs were nonplussed and Thomas - our 17-year old senior citizen cat from Omsk - gave out a scornful "Pshaw!" and then looked the other way. Somehow it had the feel of permanence about it, and before long Mandarin had more or less moved in. I say 'more or less' because he would never stay put. He had his feral heart, remember, and he liked the nightlife of the fields. So after sleeping in our house all day, usually nuzzled in between the drowsing dogs that sprawled on pillows on the bed in my office, he would stand up, arch his back like a young Mozart off to play a concerto, and ask to be let out. It got so he would sit on one of the patio chairs and cast his green eyes about the air until the darkness fell, then suddenly jump down and dart to the edge of the property, standing there like a spy taking mental notes, and then be whisked away by his own urges, our tawny zephyr, into the yawning meadow. He would be gone, and that's all we would see of him until the next morning. Lithe and lost, our fleet meadow mouse.

The dogs and Thomas and I wake up at 5.30 AM, and, while Mandarin existed, we would tumble downstairs together to have a quick bite to eat before the dog-walk, Mandarin would be there on the patio chair, and would rush in as soon as I opened the door. He would roll on his back to signal submission and compliance (his strategic ploy to placate the canines), then dart upstairs, exercise his claws on the carpet for a moment, then rush into Liuba's bed after a snack from the bowl of dry food that would always be full. That was the routine. I was kind of hoping it would last forever, and a small part of me was expecting it might.

The problem, you see, was whether or not to *force* Mandarin to become a house cat by whatever means necessary - such as just keeping him shut up inside - or to accept the inevitable, which was that Mandarin would never be happy like that. So what to do… put him under house arrest for *our sake* or leave him to his own devices, knowing full well that running free could amount to a dodgy, dicey life, maybe even the fulfillment of what actually struck me as a freedom-propelled feline death wish?

We chose freedom for Mandarin. Maybe it would have been different had we been living in our apartment back in Moscow. But out here in the bulrushes, it would have been absurd to force a feral cat with wildness in his heart to live like an old, crazed Howard Hughes or a young reclusive Emily Dickinson. Also, it would have been easier, one way or other other, if both Liuba and I had not fallen in love with this strange, fragile, but fiercely independent little sprite. It's always hell when you fall in love with something that seems bent on self-destruction…

The transitional spring-to-summer month of June has come, and after a spell of unseasonably cold weather in May, things are hotting up. But there is sporadic rain also, and when that happens the grass and weeds shoot up like the penises of the Roman army at the sight of Cleopatra.

Lately I have watched the bald and empty patches of the land fill with marching armies of green rifles and turn into leafy long-limb battalions. What it was in February - the charred starkness of the hillocks when the winter plowing was done and hard winds blew and the herd of cows was driven daily by their swain to feed on the still clumpy grasses below — has given way now to a wild and uncontrolled fecundity. In February and March, buttoned to the teeth to drive the frost away, I could move the dogs around vast areas, also way up into the hills. But it is now changed into an untended legion of verdant and discordant spikes and tentacles: olive -green, bronze-green, Prussian green, bottle-green, pea-green, apple-green, forest-green, too much of a good thing, so much it could strangle you...because the village authorities have neither means nor will to trim the landscape down, and so even the paths are growing over. One of those I normally use is now all but impassable unless I bat it with my mountain man walking stick, and in the mornings all is drowning in dew, so we come home soaked - me from the waist down and the dogs completely.

Into this miasma, Mandarin would disappear at night. And now in that jungle are found the summer snakes, some poisonous, some not, and at night the hungry, gnarly, troll-like forest dogs venture closer to the village lights and the surrounding unofficial garbage dumps, their voices synchronized into an ear-splitting complaint, like the drill of a mad dentist in a nightmare, while the moon, bulbous or in profile, looks on,
pock-marked, brainless.

So the summer jungle is full of traps, and Mandarin, even with proper feeding and care, is as light as a whisper, and no match at all for many of the enemies he might find out there. And now he has been gone too long. I fear him dead, but some people I know insist that cats with his background can return at any moment. I had thought about having him castrated at one point, thinking that might settle him down. I could have *made* him stay with us. But it wouldn't have been right that way.

For some reason, as I try to invent alternative outcomes for Mandarin other than the death he has probably died, I have been thinking about a neighbor and classmate of mine many years ago. His name was Harold Cavender, and he lived up in the hills on a dead-end street above my own dead-end in Charleston, West Virginia. He was a handsome boy — not an athlete like I was — but, as I recall, wiry and springy, olive-skinned, light-boned like Mandarin, not effeminate at all, but manly...like Mandarin... and fresh-faced. He had a sister with the odd name of Dreama. He liked the girls and they liked him, although we were much too young then to do anything but ogle and flirt.

As it turned out, ogling and flirting was all it would ever be for Harold. By the time we reached our senior year in high school, I was already living in Minnesota with my Mom and newly acquired stepdad. This was 1966 and I had really upset the applecart by starting to date a black girl from my school. My white brethren weren't happy, community pressure was applied, ugly phone calls began arriving in the middle of the night, and so my grandparents - with whom I had been living for 10 years - panicked, and next thing you know I was on a plane for
St. Paul, Minnesota.

Apparently, what happened to Harold was this: he was 18, it was spring of his senior year, and he was getting ready to graduate from Stonewall Jackson High School in a couple of weeks. He had been begging his folks for a motorcycle and so they bought him one as a graduation present. Stonewall was a big school on a great sloping green mound with a paved alley in the back that could be driven through by cars… or a motorbike. It's where all the cool kids would go to hang out and smoke (nobody had yet decided it was bad for your health). So Harold rode on his new chopper to the school one Saturday morning, apparently, for a practice run-through of the soon-to-be graduation ceremony, which was quite a big deal - then as now. After the practice (I wasn't there, remember; I am only imagining the scene), he hopped on his bike, probably without a helmet - this was a long time ago - and, maybe to impress the other kids - roared off like a hero, noisily whipping out from behind the building into the regular road running downhill next to the school. Well, a car was coming, and it clipped Harold, throwing him into the wall of the school building and crushing his skull. The end of Harold. Just like that.

I don't remember exactly when I heard the news. I guess one summer when I came back up from Florida to live in Charleston again for a while. I worked in a 'rehab' center for people with neck and spinal trauma, and one of my patients was a young black kid named Charlie Andrews, who had been on the wrestling squad at Stonewall and was cocky as hell until one day he was horsing around with another kid in his driveway and landed wrong and broke his neck. Quadriplegic all the way. Charlie was skinny by that time, all his golden muscle tone lost forever. He was very, very bitter and uncooperative. Poor guy. It must have been during that period that I learned about Harold.

Over the years I have thought about this boy many times. It's as though we have lived parallel lives, except that my life has been lived in life and his life has been lived in death. I know of no other way to put it.

It's not like we were best friends or anything. It's like...well, this is hard to express...but have you met people who just seemed more *alive*, more vital, than others, and had a different look in their eyes as if there was some specific reason for their being here, and not just an accident of birth? Descartes said, "I think; therefore, I am." And for me, this statement evinces not mere logic but some insatiably active, indomitable sense of self-hood, a passionate awareness of the life bursting within oneself.

To put it crudely, some people are easy to imagine as cannon fodder, nothing more than bit players who will never make a difference and whose lives and deaths will pass unnoticed like scoops of chicken feed withdrawn from a barrel in a barnyard and scattered morning after morning. Like shadows along a street. But with other people, you can never imagine them being dead because they seem so alive. They have this strange way of helping you feel safer in the world, and it makes it all the more stunning when they do die. Proof of their ephemeral mortality pulls down your own safety net.

Harold was like that. Not that he was some kind of born leader or gladiator. But there was a battery burning in his face that said, "I live in here!"

And so I can imagine his last instant of life as being full of rage and disbelief. Especially disbelief. "It can't end like this !!!!!" - and then it did, the voice torn right out of his throat…

He made one mistake. I have made a thousand mistakes. Really stupid ones, often alcohol induced, in cars, in seedy areas, in urban war zones. I have survived and ultimately become a decent man. But had I died in any of those situations I wandered into in the past, I would not have deserved the tears I know my mother would have shed. What I had, and what I still have - and what I would swear that some people seem somehow to lack - is an almost fanatical drive to survive. I am 70 now, and once in a while I hear death wheezing in my bones - I know the sound he makes - but a part of me still laughs at him.

Death is still more a theory to me than a confrontational dark angel; he is an enemy I can yet control. Or so I think when I wake up every morning. "Beat you again," I whisper, and, deep down, I simply cannot come to terms with any such nonsense as that I will vanish, I will no longer be here, I will cease to exist. Like an abracadabra speck of dying soul whirling down a lungless filter into a black hole. Not me. Not Little Eric Le Roy who once cried and sang in his mother's arms.

Nor am I swayed one way or the other by any guess or glimpse regarding an 'afterlife.' Such a vision remains as cloudy to me as a fog in the mountains, or a smoky window, or glass full of false teeth from the previous night, its water now the color of phlegm. I just think I will always survive to take the next breath, even as I am aware of the absurdity of such thinking.

Harold Cavender was the same as me in the sense that he just wasn't supposed to die like that, and he knew it very well. Unlike me, he actually did die. And so, probably because we were the same age and with the same prospects spreading out before us, I have carried Harold Cavender with me all these many years.

It's like with Mandarin. In the short time he stayed with us, he clipped many sharp and silver images right out of the thin air for us to hang in our brains. Like a gallery. Mandarin doing this, Mandarin doing that. There are countless dogs and cats, and I have never been a 'cat guy' - but Mandarin was different. I knew he was vulnerable, but I always thought he would find a way to outfox death.

And maybe he has. Maybe he found a new home. Maybe some little girl in a car driving by said "Look Mommy!" and they stopped and got him and took him to a village far away. Or maybe Mandarin fell in love and chased some female far into the forest. Maybe we'll see him again.

I think about it and wonder as I sit on the balcony and stare out into the Bliznatsi jungle which is Amazon-like in the morning, then all soft and powdery, like green talcum powder, in the bushy crepuscolo of the evening. Not long ago Mandarin was sick and we took him to the vet where it was diagnosed he had a bladder infection. Feral cats are subject to kidney disease, so we had him checked, and the vet shaved his stomach to give him an injection. As of the evening of his last departure, the fur had not grown back, and I used to stroke the thin wall of his stomach. I hope no snake has bitten him there.

And with Harold, I once wrote a short story in which I had three extended outcomes for his life. In one, he became a travelling salesman and went about the country seducing women in a purely comic way; in a second version, he got married, settled down as the owner of a small business, and had a big family; in the third, he became an entrepreneur and traveled around the world. An older Harold by then, the olive cheeks sagging a bit but still the same glittering luster in his eyes. Harold Cavender in Paris. Harold Cavender in Hong Kong. By then he liked to gamble, and it was not uncommon to see Harold in the casinos. Sort of a restless guy, this version, full of wanderlust and yet strangely unfulfilled. Many end this way: doing everything, and then dying with a profound sense of having left some action or deed of the utmost importance implausibly unfinished and never done at all.

Mandarin should be home, but he isn't, and sitting here on the balcony as evening shifts to dark has not changed anything. So I turn to Harold and say, "Damn good thing you were wearing that crash helmet, or you might not be here today. Am I right?"

And Harold Cavender - as I try to see him in the gathering dark now, I cannot make out if he is still 18 or 70, as I am - he says back to me. "You're damned right, Eric. It's a good thing I was." So, I say, "Well, let's go for a walk. We can get a beer up the road and see if that doggone cat is anywhere."

Blinking away the darkness, Harold says, "It sounds like a good idea to me. Let's go."

And together we do, we go.

O, VAPID VOYEUR, LET'S WALK IN THE RAIN

One of my teenage Russian Skype students, a very bright young fellow named Maxim, is more or less obsessed with cars. Often at the weekends he visits the Moscow dealerships just to check them out. But his interest does not go the usual route of jargon-signifying chatter about what's under the hood and snorting demands of "Does it have four-wheel drive?" Nor - at least I don't think - is he at the point yet where a car becomes a Phallic symbol.

He is a historian and, believe it or not, a connoisseur. He knows every model and where it started. Together we have watched documentaries tracing the history of Le Mans, for example, and all the technology behind the development of these rocketing machines, the dreamers who conceived of and built them, and the intrepid drivers who gunned them through the swerves and bends, many of whom were 'killed in action.'

Maxim also knows a tremendous amount about the history of American music. Because of him - he is only about 15, maybe 16 (I'll have to ask) - I now know more about this industry in my own (former) country than I did before. That means the blues, jazz, country, rock 'n' roll, and vintage pop. The kid is a walking, talking encyclopedia. If you want to learn about Miles Davis or Buddy Holly, just ask Maxim. He'll tell you. Before Max showed me, I never knew there were so many great documentaries about this fertile (and original) aspect of American history.

Lately, Max has become interested in - of all things - the typewriter. He even went out and bought one. An older model manual one, I mean. (What would have been the point of getting an electric version? The idea was to go as far back in time as possible.) Now he is fooling around with it, getting acquainted with its feel, heft, durability, and cave man subtlety. In our last 'lesson,' starting with Johann Gutenberg's invention of the printing press, we traced together the history and development of these now 'obsolete' machines, checking out photos of typewriters going way back to their first usage in 1874. They started to become popular in offices in the 1880s, and as recently as the 1970s were still both operative and entirely necessary. Remington. Underwood. Yes, I remember those names, the way I remember the Gipper and Ruth. Also, before my time, but part of the culture. Like RCA Victor victrolas and those old radios that were as big as suitcases from which the whole world came out- not just DJs and orgiastic blabbers of gassy jabber like today.

Talk about 'memory lane.' I had never realized that I could trace my life according to my experiences with typewriters. Nor that these particular machines could suddenly come to life again for me in terms of trying to articulate both the good and bad sides of the past and its old ways, its formulas now mostly set aside for attics and dim drawers. Of course, telephone booths, drive-in movies, jukeboxes, pinball machines, and the clotheslines that used to fill the backyards of America, sheets flapping like a chain-mail of doves and drying underwear that revealed the size of every ass in the house - all gone.

Life was more tactile back then.

Let me put it this way. I deal a lot with young Russian IT people, and I am pretty sure that young IT people are about the same the world over. They are into the 'new' realities, which is something of an oxymoron when you consider that the cyberspace regions they inhabit are *not* real. But then again, they *are* to the warriors that wander there, the inhabitants who are more at home there than anywhere else. They will tell you it's better there, like someone who has left rainy England to go live in
sunny Australia.

If you do the latter - move to Australia, it is possible, even likely, that the time will come when you miss the old drizzle along the bleak, stony English lanes, sodden green rolling away on either side if not hemmed in by hedges as stiff and rigid as an English aristocrat's portrait, which in turn bring back memories of some old love you used to meet in one of the pubs along those lanes. For, as the poet states, "Nostalgia comes with the smell of rain, you know."

But if you grow up in Australia, you will not miss English rain. How can you, if you never knew it? Maybe it's possible, but only for those blessed with a certain intensity of imagination. In that case, one can grow nostalgic in the deepest sense...for what never existed. A paradox, but true. I myself have always been in love the most with invisible women whose voices fill the choruses of the light night radio.

My IT students do not believe that it could ever be possible to rush out into the yard during a sudden shower and bring the still half-dry clothes in from the rain. It was the world of their grandparents. They see no point in putting on layers of clothing during the Russian winter to go grocery shopping when it is simpler just to use the smart phone to order the food and have it delivered. Why push and drag a vacuum cleaner around the apartment or house when you can purchase a robot?

We accepted remote control for the TV and dinner prepared by microwave long ago (or so it seems. Maybe it wasn't that long ago.). Electric toothbrushes to keep us from having to move our hands up and down. Electric hair dryers. The smartphone that now tells us everything...

So, these new realities call for abandoning, little by little, the old realities. Just as old people die and are replaced by new ones. Each batch of people had and have their own sets of tools and toys, and parts of life must always remain simply inscrutable each to each, while, on a different level, every generation dreams the dream and finds what glory there may be amid the greater grief and the inevitable ruins. *Il tempo passa per tutti.*

The big difference is the way in which the gadgets spearhead our gallop through life, ever faster and faster. They save time, I am told. If so, this is a very good thing indeed, since many of my IT friends claim to work 12-14 hours per day. Or would it be closer to the truth to suggest that such gizmos and all the technology behind them only *appear* to save time - but in fact serve more to create labyrinth after labyrinth of tantalizing possibility, as if secretly whispering to their addicted users, "Don't shut us off now! We have more surprises!?" And at 3 a.m. the surprises just keep coming.

We have so many friends, all of them only a click away. It's pretty awesome if you ask me. And, gee, they are all such great and lasting friends... just a click away. And don't they just respond so faithfully to our Instagram and Facebook posts? That's how they prove their friendship, and I knew it when I lived in Moscow myself and received 'likes' even from those who lived a few metro stops from me and I saw in real life maybe twice in five years. I never doubted their loyalty.

That's why watching those documentaries about typewriters last week made me remember all the miserable hours I used to spend trying to get something typed. I was error-prone, you see (as in life). Plus, being self-taught, I never learned how to do it (type) using all my digits, but only the index fingers on each hand (which remains my keyboard technique to this day). Sure, it got so I could fly along at a good clip, but I was never 'secretary' material. Problems, problems.

It would start with just putting the paper in straight, which for me was always a chore. If it was a term paper for school, I would have to add in the footnotes at the bottom of each page (all the 'ibids' and 'op cits'). This meant calculating how much room was needed. Failure to accurately estimate the space would mean your citation running off the end of the page, which in turn meant retyping the whole thing. In retrospect, I believe that my mental illness problems started with typing the same page 15 times. It will do that to you.

The typewriter had a ribbon where the ink that went on the page came from. As the ribbon started to get old, the impression on the hammered page would grow fainter and fainter until you had to pound on the keys like you were trying to break down your ex-wife's door - in order to make an impression on the parchment. When a new ribbon was installed, you had to be careful not to smear the fresh ink on your fingers, which would, of course, transfer to anything else you touched, be it your nose or your dick.

Mistakes. Ah, yes, there were plenty. To eradicate them, all we had in the beginning was a special kind of 'type eraser' stuck on the end of what otherwise just looked like a plain pencil and which would remove the ink slowly and painfully. To visualize the process, imagine a trapped animal gnawing off its own paw in order to escape the clutches of the steel jaws. If you got impatient and rubbed too hard, you can guess what would happen: you would bore a hole right through the damned paper. After a minute or two of staring murderously at the wall, you would simply have to insert another sheet and begin again. There was no other way.

Then, as God is always providing us with in times of dire straits, a miracle came along. This was called 'liquid paper.' It arrived in small bottles - like nail polish and it had the same sharp smell. You just unscrewed the lid, pulled it off, and you would find that a dainty little brush was attached. You dipped it (not too much!) in the magic white 'milk' and gently applied it to the page where your error had occurred. If you weren't too blind to see what you were doing or shaking too much from the previous night's under-the-table piss-up, and if you laid it on j-u-s-t right, then the error disappeared and you could start again. Unless, you forgot to give it about 20 seconds to dry. If you started typing right away, it would smear just like kissing a woman (or whoever) wearing fresh lipstick.

The liquid paper would work like a dream… for a while. Until it gradually started to thicken, which it always did. Then it was like... goo. Or the snot produced by a particularly bad cold. Or bubble gum. The result was a turgid, mucked up mess that the typing key could even get stuck in and have to be manually removed. It was especially heartbreaking when something irretrievably screwed up and draft-ruining happened near the bottom of a carefully wrought page of copy. If it was a personal manuscript, okay. You could just forgive yourself for the butchered aesthetics and push on. But if it was intended for a finicky prof, you couldn't have it looking like somebody with black lung disease had just sneezed all over the page. You had to do it again.

My rage-torn room was always full of wadded up discards. Indeed, it was how I perfected the art of verbal *filth,* moving from one word expletives to combinations as deft as a figure skater and versatile as a break dancer. Whole lyrics and soliloquies of the slimiest and vilest language the English tongue is capable of came boiling from my mouth as if I were inventing Hell right there and then in my pauper's garret.

Somehow, I always got my assignments done, and even wrote quite a large section of a never-completed novel. And lots of other stuff, mostly poetry and love letters to women with cold hearts. I didn't feel oppressed or put upon, because the typewriter, as a piece of equipment, was as good as it seemed like it was going to get in those days. And when electric typewriters came along to replace the manual ones, I thought that technology (we didn't use that word back then) had reached its zenith.

I can remember living in Bath, England, and carrying a massive old Underwood up six flights of stairs to my bed-sitter (one room 'studio apartment') in Green Park, then sitting up nights with flagons of cider banging away, banging away, clickety-clack, clickety-clack, well into the witching hours of the gloaming, sometimes with a lover already asleep in the bed near my desk, but often alone, writing poetry and dreaming that I would become the next Eliot or Yeats.

Then came the word processors and computers, and almost overnight typewriters disappeared faster than the Knights Templar or a pickpocket in the plaza. The typewriter went the way of silent films and the Brooklyn Dodgers. To be honest, I wasn't unhappy, not a bit.

Until the other evening with Maxim when together we looked through photos of those old machines - the photos looking as grey and dreary and smudge-worn as the old typewriters themselves. But then...a revelation.

It turns out that some authors still use typewriters, just as some continue to write their texts in pen and pencil. Their explanation was simple - and it is the same one used by people who still prefer real books to electronic ones. They prefer the tactile. The physical element. They don't want to save the planet or recycle their environment so much as they just want to touch and taste and feel and smell and listen to the Sounds of Life.

It's not - as the IT people might justifiably believe - that such people are just holding on...and how silly...to a past that is no more alive than an ashtray that someone forgot to empty after last night's party. Nor is it, in many cases, just a matter of anti-social stubbornness and hidebound hoarfrost.

Think about it - okay, play the romantic for a moment - maybe it's about people - lovers maybe - who would rather walk home in the rain, arriving completely soaked and yet...somehow...exhilarated, and feeling strangely better for having done so - when the easy solution would have been to grab that taxi sitting nearby. Then ask yourself this simple question based on the scenario I have described: a young couple come in and fling off their wet clothes, glistening in their translucent ivory or ebony nakedness, hair gleaming with rainwater and hurry (maybe) under the shower together before dissolving into each other's arms in bed...

VS

...the two in the taxi who come in completely dry and distracted by pressing appointments and tasks, tasks, and more tasks awaiting them in the late hours after work at the business 'park,' who simply remove their coats, not needing each other now, and immediately start switching switches and punching buttons. And go about their labor and their toil... meticulously, purposefully, silently, sullenly. In the same room, a universe apart.

Which life do you want? Woody Allen (fuck whether or not you like Woody Allen as a human being) captures this perfectly in his film "Midnight in Paris." The protagonist cannot, CANNOT get his stupid girlfriend to go for a walk in the Parisian rain, and why is that? Because to her, it is ONLY rain, and nothing else. She cannot - because she is too brain dead and materialistic - see the rain, not just as rain, but as metaphor. METAPHOR. But, by disappearing back in time (see the film) he finally finds a girl who will walk with him in the rain. And he never wants to come back to that rainless world and rainless woman that was his 'holiday' and 'fiancee.'

The people who see life as metaphor as always, virtually without exception, are the smartest people and the ones who live the fullest lives.

And so the man who still prefers his typewriter to the keyboard, is not backward or clueless, at least not necessarily. Maybe he is seeing the typewriter as a metaphor for something else - for a way of life which somehow keeps him c-o-n-n-e-c-t-e-d to something he senses is valuable, maybe even precious, and which holds more meaning for him than any quick-fix alternative. He wants to touch life, feel life, smell and taste life - not just as a RESULT but as a PROCESS.

He doesn't want 50 Starbucks choices of 'java' any more than he wants 50 Haagen Daz flavors of ice cream. He wants to *taste* simple black, well-brewed coffee maybe with a real shot of cream in it -- a fresh dollop! - and a simple tasty, fulsome lump

of a-u-t-h-e-n-t-i-c ice cream. NOT the frozen semen out of a Dairy Queen contraption.
Just as I would venture, he wants to *taste* his friendships. He wants to be in the same room with these people and walk down the streets and through the dawn and the darkness with them. Wake up on the same floor with them after a huge birthday or New Year's Eve party.

This is what the cyberspace people cannot understand. O, they may wake up on the floor the next morning too, but basically they miss the point, just as the man or woman who prefers to order food on a smartphone rather than get up and go and get it fails to understand.

This sad person wants only results. They have forgotten- or never known, which is likely the case today - that the journey counts for more than the result.

Go into the street, meet the people of the wind and the rainy day people of the lanes and avenues and come back, yes, straining with your bags of food and yes, yes, yes, muttering because the wind is cold and sharp, and say hello to that old woman walking her dog, that skulking cat on the fence post, that old man on the stairs, and maybe that pretty girl out on the landing.

Say hi to the drunk in front of the metro and drop a coin in his grubby but grateful hand, pause and listen to that teenager playing classical violin in the frosty evening (I have), watch the cop chasing an illegal immigrant down into the metro, stroke the fur of the lonely but free stray dog on the street, say hello to one and all, pull down your vanities and say hello.

When you get home you will feel better, and the beer will taste better than if you never went out. Much better than if they had just brought it to your door. And if you live in a place where there is no elevator and you have to walk up, rejoice. Leonardo da Vinci and Galileo had to walk up the stairs too. There were no lifts.

That's why the old typewriters were worth their salt. You could feel them. You beat on them, and goddamned if they didn't mess with you in return. Like they knew you and were laughing at you.

Cyberspace doesn't laugh. It just consumes.

It appears that young Maxim, as if listening to some old jukebox in a roadside diner, or maybe just the voices of the wind, understands this in the way that roosters know when to crow and wolves howl at the edges of the forest.

PHANTOM FRIENDS AMID NIGHT MUSIC

People are like stories. If the story is interesting and keeps you spellbound as it turns its depths to you, then you want to keep reading. If it starts to be dull, especially when the outcome seems predictable, then you put it down. It happens too when you don't believe the story. In literature classes, this is called a violation of 'the suspension of disbelief." Coleridge said it, I believe.

People are also like stories in the sense that all of us, one way or another, are mere fiction - inventions of our own dreaming as we try to fit our fantasies around ourselves like leotards in the summer, and warm hats and gloves in winter. If it all feels successful, then we shop ourselves around to see if there are any takers.

If we reach a point with other people where they stop making us want to keep turning the pages, we can put down the book and walk away. Either the fiction got stale, or we didn't believe it anymore. But interesting falsehood is not always so terrible, don't you agree? We have to survive one way or another. And we have our reputations to protect.

Memory works like this, too. As time wears on, we choose past versions of our lives which, if not really based on fact, nevertheless seem to capture the essence of whatever we have always needed to believe about ourselves and each other. Think of some dark gallery which we have filled with rows of self-portraits painted in our dreams. We are tempted to go there in the heart of the afternoon when everything is bright and the vivid oils on the canvasses almost start to bubble as if fires were burning behind them. But we don't. We really don't need to see those garish sights stripped of their protective shadows. The dark is safer, We huddle in our mental wombs and give birth to image after image. There we find, not the secrets of creation, but the ways of creation's choreography. In this respect, all of us are illusionists, nothing more. In this manner we fake our lives.

No need to be ashamed: we all do it. I am not speaking of the boldfaced lies that swaying men in barrooms tell yarns about: Heroism in wars never fought in; tumultuous orgasms when the object of desire was never present; conversations with God when one never did more than drop a few coins into a hat that swept along the pews.

I am speaking about necessary lies, the ones we use to keep our sanity.

I invent myself and offer it to you, and you do the same to me. It's like being in a restaurant and both of us need to visit the toilet. We don't discuss what we plan to do; it is obvious, and, besides, one simply doesn't announce that he is going to sit on a bowl and shit. But maybe a secret phone call has to be made. Or one needs to slip out the back door for a hidden reason. So we grant each other these moments of darkness, these small eternities of 'in-between', like actors hurrying around backstage. It's like a quick trip into outer space. Or Clark Kent changing into Superman and then into Clark Kent again. A step off the face of the earth to do a little business. Then it's back to the world of appearances.

In my selection of friends, lovers, even wives (by which I mean that they in turn selected me, too, or I would have spent a lot of time talking to myself!), I have always made room for the fact that all I will ever know about these people is what they want me to know and most of that has been derived from lying to themselves. Shadows fascinate me - I mean the shadows in people. It's not that I want to be a fly buzzing around the room when people I barely know are naked, gape through peepholes, or stand outside the door and listen while they are humming to themselves, or pulling their pudding or praying. Life need not obsess with investigative journalism (I once found out that a woman I asked out to lunch had done a background check on me before accepting. I thought it was a bit much before taking a chance on a cheeseburger!)

Women have tiptoed through my dusky thoughts for years, but lived and died centuries ago. What if they came striding out of the real shadows this afternoon? Would 30 minutes be enough to shatter images they created many centuries ago, which are the reasons I have loved them? Would it be ruined, all ruined, and would my inner sirens cry out "What the Fuck was THAT all about???"

In real life, many love affairs - or so my opinion runs - last in earnest only as long as the illusion lasts. Many people (maybe even me included) are incapable of loving anything that is not fashioned by their own imagination. They/we grab hold of a fantasy and drape that fantasy over the shoulders of another person. If the person looks good in the mantle and wears it well, a magic spell is cast. 'Love' endures while the magic spell endures. It leads one to the conclusion that the lover adores the object of his attention only as long as 'it' remains an extension of himself. When this object breaks off the dance and stands alone as a truly separate being, the lover is aghast.

He feels cheated. It never occurs to him what a monster he is. Yet, he is not a ghoul, and neither am I, who also have been guilty of projecting my make-believe worlds onto others who have no obligation to respond. A mild monster, let's leave it at that.

I have wondered what goes through the mind of a true psychopath. What did guys like Ted Bundy really think about while they were just sitting in a movie house watching a film? Or eating spaghetti at Pizza Hut? Who were these gargoyles who could dress up like lawyers? And those we regard as saints? Monks who lived in stony dents atop high cliffs...did they always just think about God? Did Jesus masturbate? (He would have to have existed, of course.) How truly different were these people who dwell on the distant fringes from you and me? Most of us tame our demons, and otherwise erect taboos we would never violate, but I think (I believe this, though maybe it is only indicative of my corrupted nature) that in every soul there are strangers wandering around the bus stations of bleak, drab cities, scooping cigarettes butts up from the snot-and-spit-frosted concrete floors. There is an executioner in each of us, and there is a hanged corpse. And in every one of us, as C.S. Lewis wrote, "There is a Godlike void."

These people are our friends, lovers, wives and husbands. We just don't know them well enough.

"Tu le connais, lecteur, ce monstre délicat. ("You know him, reader, this exquisite monster.)
Hypocrite lecteur, — mon semblable, — mon frère!" —
(Hypocrite reader — my twin — my brother!")
© Charles Baudelaire

But it's not altogether true what Baudelaire wrote. We share vices and virtues. Not souls.

Friends. I used to think that, well, friends were those things that everyone has, like two ears and an asshole. One lived; one made friends. Like going to the supermarket to buy apples. Or walking around in a field where leaves were shaking in the big winds of early spring and some of them just cascaded over you like an emerald ticker tape parade. It wasn't complicated at all, and, moreover, it was the birthright of small-town America when I was growing up. Your next-door neighbor didn't have much else to do, and so he became your friend. And the next thing you knew, 50 years later, you were serving as his pallbearer down at the cemetery (if you didn't find your way into a box first). In between, what had transpired? Probably not much. Or maybe you were secretly working against each other. Did it matter? Maybe you even grew to quietly hate each other. Maybe you were jealous and covetous. Maybe you imagined taking a machine gun and wasting the bastard in the middle of a church service. This was also the meaning of 'friends'. I am sure these definitions have stood the test of time. That's why the late writer Gore Vidal said, "When a friend succeeds, something in me dies." And it's why someone else said, "It is easier to forgive an enemy than a friend."

I live in a village now. I had lots of acquaintances in Moscow. Now I have them all on Skype. Everywhere: China (especially), Korea, Japan, the Netherlands, Brazil, Chile, Peru, and, of course Russia. I have become used to the disembodied aspect that comes from talking to human heads on a computer all day - I teach English to people I will never see three-dimensionally. But it doesn't appear that all that much is lost. A phantom is a phantom. I know one guy that I actually have a cyberspace beer party with now and then. He drinks his in Moscow, I drink mine here. We laugh and cut the monkey as before. There is not one iota of difference between the real man and the ghost. Which is troublesome, when you think about it.

When I came here from Moscow, I had faint, blinking illusions of finding one of those quaint places lost from the world's map where 'simple' actually meant 'simplicity', and it would be like the best of the big city distilled into some shaggy-treed meadow-laden vista, a mixture of hills and valleys, where predator and prey involved themselves in an endless game of hide and seek and no actual blood was ever spilled, yet both flew back to their nests well-fed and satiated. And in the middle of it all would be this pub that opened in the evenings like a blinking star, and charming eccentric people or local farmers with roughened hides and the masculine workmen's hands I have always envied went to dry their sweat with grog and mock all things evil with mirthful anecdotes. The stalwart dogs would be waiting outside, sitting on their haunches with their ears perked, and beyond them the blank-eyed cows of the silver-dark hours, heavy with milk, waiting for the summoning sound of the evening bells. Friends like fattened cream That would be the village.

It's not like that at all. Villages are 'set pieces' where people made up their minds about everything a long time ago. They are friendly enough, but their lives are closed; there are no street festivals and no one bakes pies for the newcomers. My next door neighbor speaks only Bulgarian, but he understands Russian, and he is a nice man. Yevo, his name, or so it sounds in English. At New Year I give him champagne and he gives me his homemade rakia, which my wife quickly confiscates: I never taste a drop of it. Russian women from the provinces have one mission in life, and that is to keep their husbands sober. I have become friends with Yevo's dog Hatchek, a huge German Shepherd.

Gypsies, much despised by many but not by me, slither about the village. Most of them sell wood for the winter fires. My wife chases them away, but when I see them at the shop where I buy bread and milk and beer, I go out of my way to be friendly. Not used to being liked, they are the most cheerful people I have met here, and I have never been able to decide if their eyes are really that open and almost tender, or if it is just a matter of their being cunning and scheming. Village girls - sorry romantics! - are not comely like city girls, at least as urbanites (often transplanted village girls) are before the city gets to them too much. But after a while, maybe because there's nothing else to see, they start to look better. I have always found wherever I go that after a certain time you start to identify beauty in the faces at hand. They are women of the universe and would know how to please, even exquisitely, if you went with them. Some things come naturally.

In late spring the Brits arrive, pink as late-stage pimples, and as openly friendly as the doors of spring. Invariably likable, a lot of them own property here. They are good for the chat and the bevy. A bit superficial. But better than nothing.

The beauty here lies in the landscape and the sky. Both are always changing. In the mornings lately I have watched the tightly wound flocks that seem like specks of black gravel someone flung up into the air. They are heading south to Turkey and Greece, I think. Forest dogs wail in the night. The roosters crow in the morning. Sometimes the furtive owl appears in the belfry opposite me.

The city was all about quick. Quick hellos, quick decisions, quick sex, quick goodbyes. The joy, such as it was, came from the sudden-silver anonymity that is the nature of the megapolis. There, the truly fictive brand of friendship and romance continues, albeit impassively in its non-heart, to flourish in the name of fantasy. A good story is all you need to Be - someone who can make others wish to keep turning your pages for a while - a fluttering murmur - and you will sift through their pages as well. It is like a mutual massage in some windy Japanese studio where two-dimensional paintings adorn the walls. There is nothing beyond those skies. Eventually in life, one arrives at the plain existential truth that there is nothing beyond any of it, and you do not expect anything else.

I believe that big city lovers are happiest that way. They have forgotten what bindings they lack, to steal a line from that great Cyndi Lauper song.

Sometimes my wife, who wakes up late, wanders by the door to my bedroom office and sees me talking with great animation, usually waving my arms. I am confirmed in my apelike gesticulations like an Italian stereotype in a Hollywood movie. When I talk to my much revered colleague-in-arms Petr with whom I am in ongoing-disagreement-always-reconciled-as-soon-as-we-finish-the-call relationship, my wife must think (I wear headphones, so she can't hear what my students are saying), that my antics betray the insanity she often attributes to me. She must think I am pacing some imaginary cage like a circus animal gone berserk. To her I am a lunatic who gets paid by sympathetic offerings, like an abandoned child being cared for by deer and wolves.

She has been taking piano lessons for several months now and is beginning to show improvement. The dogs and I often sit on the sofa opposite the fireplace (always ablaze these winter evenings) and listen to her melodies, evoked with halting fingers and joined only now and then by the beginnings of full, crunching chords. I think I can speak for the dogs (and the cat also) if I say that we are enchanted.

But even better, she has begun to paint, and this is her real talent. She has primitive genius. Her work is prodigious, and it awakens me. After 10 years I had begun to look at her with complacency. Now I behold her with awe. Maybe she is that much better than me, moving beyond into some dream field and Sargasso Sea where I don't belong. Like a wind amid geraniums, I shake my head. I look at my wife with wonder.

She always says we should have met earlier. Imagine if our lives (and deaths) were that way. Imagine if we lived from back to front. That we got up out of our graves and moved backwards into life and further, earlier life. We would meet our memories. Moreover, we would meet the motives behind these memories. Like reading a book. We would see all the little clues that led to later things. We would see our mothers and fathers when they were young. Probably, in that way, we could better forgive them for getting old and dying.

I have a trace of Jewish blood in me. Not much, but a drop or two. I confess I love the Jews. They have suffered and the bitterness remains. They have been identified as crafty usurers and devious opportunists, and maybe they have been. But Jewish comedy and science and art and music, tokens of an endless capacity for life - suffused with wit and grief - seem to me to lift Jewish existence out of the mire. For a long time I have wished I were a Jew. I even asked one of my best Russian-Jewish friends in Moscow: "How do I become a Jew?" I thought he would send me a manual, a prayer book, maybe the Talmud, and directions to a synagogue. Instead, he said you become a Jew by being a Jew in your heart. And he said that I identified with Jews because I had always been left out in the cold. He said you are a Jew if you want to be; you don't need to do anything else.

So many nights I sit up here on the balcony where it is cold indeed. The fireplace burns below, but when it goes out, you would be surprised how quickly penetrating the chill becomes. Then I sit, vindictively in my robe, sneering at the absurdity of the world, almost crying because I need the kindness of the world so much, and I think of people I would like to write to, people I was with once and whose faces time has robbed as it has robbed my own. Come back, come back. Come… back…

But like many wicked people, my mind contains the observant avarice of a card shark. A sensual wildness electrocutes my blood, eyes gleaming with sentimental animosity… I am an Old Jew. Leave me alone to suffer, I say.

In my sincerity I feel Insincerity. When I am NOT lying, I feel that I must actually be doing so, against my will. From my balcony the night-dogs, the hungry, almost deformed forest curs, squeal and shriek, which sets my own healthy, home-based and staunch hounds a-howling. Which one would I be, if one were to choose among dogs? I, of the feral heart. The stray? The lost canine? Or the well-informed, domestic animals whose eyes search my eyes as if reading maps?

I practice sanity. And then my wife down below starts to touch the piano with her full-bodied late middle-aged magnificent fingers. They strain to find the right notes the way my own stiff hands do in the gelid, glittering mornings when I am trying to lace up my shoes to walk the dogs. This is not Chopin. Liubov is not there yet and won't be for a while. But she has the right idea, maybe even the right instinct. Simple, melodic notes climb the stairs. They shut down my obsessions and vanities.

But her paintings speak of the inner angels and devils that Botitcelli and Vermeer surely felt. If her paintings are not that good yet, they come from the same windy fields of the soul. I see it. Even if I can't do it, I know it. It's as clear as the one smiling face you see leaving some vague, grey, indistinct place amid a sea of furious frowns.

I see that I have borrowed another night from God.

At this moment I feel Human Warmth which pervades the peasant-simple, halting, but oddly accomplished melodies that my wife's fingers turn into art. They mount in my mind like someone making his way slowly up the hillside of a distant country, a place where things are done differently than anything you ever knew before. There are lambs on that hillside and from the farms come girls I will never know. Ah, such splendid stories lost!!! But somehow the stairway in my own house seems full of everyone I ever loved. Tonight. The ghosts are dancing, and in the air above the stairs it is if I can taste a springtime that will never end.

That's all in my mind, of course. On the balcony, I smoke one last cigarette and stare into the fog that hovers around this nocturnal hour, and it makes me want, in some way, to hold the hand of my worst enemy and throw my damned ego into the trash forever.

I want more chances to live.

So my mind is full of Jews and gypsies and wives and dogs, and everyone who has ever suffered. Suffered inexplicably, suffered because God didn't show up like you begged him to. Suffered because there was no one there to play the piano, even in a halting way, fingers searching for the right keys, and making sweet noises that float up to me. Or suffered at my hands.

Given that last, and most unsettling, maybe even stabbing, regret, this tinkling night music for me and the tame little mice in my soul that run freely now, seem like a strange form of forgiveness. Can it be? Before dreams?

I sit here, a typical human monstrosity, wanting the forgiveness of a universe that seems empty except for the music my wife provides with her artful fingers.

NOT TO WASTE YOUR LIFE

In America, guys approaching or just past 40 (in Russia it is 30, according to my friends) are always having what is known as "the mid-life crisis." I never had it because I never grew up and never wanted to deal with anything as boring as 'adult responsibilities.' Well, I jest, but maybe it says something about me that for my last Happy New Year gifts, I received a new bicycle and boxing gloves (I will be 69 on 8 May).

Alas, the sober truth is that I am having my mid-life crisis now. It probably doesn't mean that I will live to be 138; however, I notice for the first time that my elbows ache like hell after a long weight-lifting workout; same with knees and ankles. Too many years spent jumping up and down at basketball. Also, my stomach keeps ballooning out. Mostly flatulence and bloat, and I don't know which is worse: farting all the time or just getting fat. So I am taking pills to alleviate the gas. Charming, huh?

Other than that, and the fact that I get grumpy when the weather is cold, I am in great shape. So there is no crisis, right?"

O sages standing in God's holy fire
as in the gold mosaic of a wall,
come from the holy fire, perne in a gyre,
and be the singing-masters of my soul.
Consume my heart away, sick with desire
and fastened to a dying animal
it knows not what it is; and gather me
into the artifice of eternity.

© W. B. YEATS. "SAILING TO BYZANTIUM"

So. Sick with desire and fastened to a dying animal, huh? Maybe there is a problem (sorry, a 'challenge') after all? But my own has more to do with making allowances for the inevitable in the context of fully enjoying a life that has turned out relatively well. This despite many early indications that it would not.

I live in a world of self-imposed stress because I want it that way. I am, effectively, still in Moscow because it remains the source of all my business. The only difference is that Moscow now sits in my office here in this village, rather than me being in Russia and riding trains and running up and down the city every day. I joke with people that "I am too busy to get sick" or "too busy to die." Gallows humor, to be sure, but I sort of mean it. I am just sorry that my 'heart' (spirit), which is so abundant in its desire to live on and on, is indeed "fastened to a dying animal."

It's so much better now than when I was a young man, dancing drunkenly on a tabletop, splashing booze into everyone's face, and imagining this meant that I was a POET. And if, as the mirror tells me all too often, I am no longer a bargain for the young ladies, suffice it to say that I am now a better man. The psychologists call it, I believe, 'self-actualization.' That's what I have achieved somewhere along the way. The other thing it means is that I am free to die without losing my sanity because of failing to live the life I was given.

And that's where I think this mid-life crisis business kicks in with many men. As for women, I cannot say. It would be easy to dismiss their side of the coin by saying that it's all about when they start to lose their looks and sex appeal (assuming they had it in the beginning). But the world has changed, and I think that for women it's a lot more complicated than a case of the bloom going off the rose. Besides, both sexes can keep up appearances now for much longer than in the past. Credit better nutrition, better health care, more attention to fitness, cosmetic surgery, and the decision (which impacts women especially) not to reproduce so early or so often.

With men, it was always a matter of baldness setting in, a complacent-looking paunch perching itself just above the belt buckle, and fear of losing virility. Also, we should factor in the age-old notion about man being the 'hunter', the guy who was supposed to go out there and 'make it happen' while his good old gal kept the fires burning at home. Feminists pooh-pooh this idea now, but it was true for thousands of years, and I doubt that ANY woman - even a card-carrying Feminist - would be proud of having a male "significant other" or "partner" (as they say nowadays) who, being called upon to defend her against a would-be rapist, would offer to suck the guy's dick instead. Just to keep the peace.

How do you tell a bird it can't fly? When a man who in the past has thought himself a tad more than adequate suddenly or gradually (doesn't matter) has a traumatic experience or succession of deflating mini-experiences which inform him that he is no longer the meatloaf of the marketplace, it can really do a number on him. To make matters worse, this harrowing realization may coincide with his wife's indifference to his advances. Let's face it: if we are going to talk about marriage, the word 'boredom' cannot be left out of the conversation. Or maybe she is too busy with the baby. Or maybe her own jets need firing and she's on the prowl herself.

Anyway, he's worried that he's over-the-hill, and so what does he need to do? Prove himself! And how can he do that? Have an affair of course! But not just with ANYONE. I mean, since he is trying to prove something urgent not just to a woman but to himself, he must secure a CONQUEST! But since it's a Mid-Life Crisis we are talking about, it won't do to have a roll in the hay with his wife's fat cousin or pay for a rub-and-tug at the local massage cabin. No. He must win the heart of a young woman! He will pay, of course, but since men realize that they are always going to pay one way or the other, he rationalizes it, writes it off as a donation on behalf of his newly rediscovered youth, vim and vigor, O Holy Erection! And that's about the sum total of a mid-life crisis, right?

I don't think so. I think it's about something deeper and far more painful than whether or not you can bed your secretary (excuse me, Personal Assistant). Many men, including myself, who can summon up a hardness in his 'member' upon demand, is left afterwards to deal with the impotence that rules his soul. I think it has to do with the creeping angst that occurs - and clings like one of the blood-sucking ticks that fasten themselves onto the country dogs out here where I live. This angst that accompanies your growing awareness of yourself as being precariously positioned in a disposable culture - one whom the city billboards constantly shout at, demanding you look up at images displaying everything you are NOT. A culture that worships youth and pays no heed to voices of experience. It is the shattering epiphany that exposes and sneers at your irrelevance. Now half your life is gone, and you are...WHO? You are WHAT? (Sorry, we can't H-E-A-R you!!! WHO?")

But maybe the crisis comes about, not from the silent sound and subtle fury that wants to bury you under the general pop culture and mass production stampede. No, maybe it's because you have not been prepared -- or prepared yourself properly - for life. Maybe it has nothing to do with your sagging tummy (or boobs) or uncooperative penis. Maybe it's because you have not prepared and built your soul in the right way.

Did I really say that? Built your soul? Yes, I guess I did. Consider this short poem which has haunted me for many years:

Over my head, I see the bronze butterfly,
Asleep on the black trunk,
Blowing like a leaf in green shadow.
Down the ravine behind the empty house,
The cowbells follow one another
Into the distances of the afternoon.
To my right,
In a field of sunlight between two pines,
The droppings of last year's horses
blaze up into golden stones.
I lean back, as the evening darkens and comes on.
A chicken hawk floats over, looking for home.
I have wasted my life.

© JAMES WRIGHT "LYING IN A HAMMOCK AT WILLIAM DUFFY'S FARM IN PINE ISLAND, MINNESOTA"

What does the author mean, what can he possibly mean "I have wasted my life"?? I have come to believe that, as the years go by, a large number of us - inflated with ego as we humans are - begin to despise ourselves, knowing, as we do, the very mean and cravenly quality of many of our underlying motives. And thus the so-called mid-life crisis comes about when the EGO, yours and mine, totters under the assault of certain unpleasant emerging realities. Existing only in the realm of competition and the Bottom Line, we are fine as long as we have our legs under us, but when something in us falters, there is no sense of harmony or serenity to come to our rescue. We rise and fall as egomaniacs.

The speaker in the poem (The poem is called "Lying in a Hammock at William Duffy's Farm in Pine Island, Minnesota") is able to see, in this privileged moment, the unadorned perfection of natural simplicity, utterly ego-free and so, to borrow from a critique by the poet Patricia Hampl, he is able to "rinse" himself (great word) of his ambitions, his pride, his shame, his grudges. He understands that he has never really seen the world before. Only his ultimately frustrating and embittering illusions. Stripped of all that burdensome gear, he becomes, at least in that moment, enlightened.

Can it be that a mid-life crisis comes about only because a man - or a woman - far from fearing the failure of his/her sexual equipment, is really caught in a seizure of angst because something in this human mechanism understands that, so far at least, he has wasted his life? And then what should he do? He should follow the cowbells into the evening?

In a sense, yes, that is exactly what he should do. Or she. The trick, I've decided after these many years, is the shedding of the ego, which some no doubt see as the lightning rod to all innovation, creation, and conquest, but which I see increasingly, especially as an older man (some may say just 'old), as the overgrown seed of our undoing. That the rat race of the world was always just that and nothing more: a vociferous onslaught of the human rodent, of those whom T.S. Eliot described thusly: "Eyes assured of certain certainties/The conscience of a blackened street/Impatient to assume the world".

Now, in these days of mass media, where everyone has a blog, a podcast, a pulpit and megaphone, we see just how desperate people are, and the more I realize (and I definitely include myself) that after all the tumult and the shouting, the sound and the fury, we are really just rather irritating passers-by on a planet that will heal itself long after we are gone.

The saddest thing is how we take some harmless little creature, a small animal maybe, and squash it in the road under the heavy tires of our cars and we hasten without reflection toward the citadels of our puniness to grab the cash. But sometimes I think that even the worst of us must feel some kind of distant regret about the things we have slaughtered along the journey, along our speedway to nowhere.

The only lasting happiness comes when we throw down our vanities and embrace humility. When we stand before the looking glass, naked in our human gown, and smile with something approaching serenity at the simultaneous miracle and absurdity of our *existence*. Take off the ego like the soul's hair-shirt and spiked collar it always was and hurl it to the ground.

And follow the cowbells into the evening. Still human, but transfigured, strangely (it will seem strange at first) until even the sound of your own name escapes you.

MEGAPOLIS

As Poppy, Casper, and I went walking in the valley near Bliznatsi Village early this morning, we came across a dead forest dog. They are small creatures and you could not describe them as beautiful - they seem almost deformed and probably lead lives of great deprivation at certain times of the year. At night, they set up a great plaintive howl in unison, and it seems they are creeping closer to our houses. This is in part because some of the less refined of the village people insist on using strips of the descending land leading to the valley and forest as their personal dumping ground. For a starving beast of the woods, rotting food probably presents a tasty-looking menu.

But it was a surprise to see this dead animal out in plain view - it must have been killed by someone ripping along the dirt stretch in a car or on a motorbike after dark, and the animal just happened to get in the way. Good guess how long it will lay there; but it won't take more than one hot afternoon for a tremendous and sickening stench to rise up out of its carcass and start to drift malignantly across the field. So the sun will defile the corpse before the partisans of sky and wood come to devour it.

The local village authorities will do nothing. They are never in a hurry to get anything done, which is why the grasses and weeds along the narrow footpath I use when walking my dogs have grown up to jungle-like dimensions. In the prodigious morning dew (we go out at 5:30), not even my high Wellington rubber boots can prevent the moisture from soaking me up to my waist and the dogs completely...

What's worse, it is 'tick' season here. Are you familiar with these creepy, miserable, voracious, parasitic motherfuckers? They jump on you and bite into your skin. With long-haired creatures they are especially treacherous. They dig in and start sucking the blood out of their host, namely dogs and cats - but they will attack people, too, if they get the chance. We have a neighbor who doesn't properly care for his big German Shepherd (keeps it chained up except for occasional short walks), and this poor dog is tick-infested. The ticks, if left unattended to their vampirish business, will swell up to the size of a human earlobe while still clinging to the animal. It's best to remove them with tweezers, so as to completely grab them by the tentacles. If you just jerk them off the dog, there is a lot of blood and their 'claws' (or whatever you would call these hellish incisors) are still gouging your 'pet'. Our own dogs and cat live in the house, so all day and before bedtime, Liuba and I give them the once-over. I actually picked one off my balls the other night. Honest. You can imagine how happy I was.

Meanwhile the mosquitoes (another of God's mistakes) hover by the doors and windows, just waiting for a chance to waft into the house and cover you with nibbling kisses... They like to announce themselves by setting off their neat little sirens in your ears right before they clamp down and tear a chunk out your hide. They are blood-suckers too. Amazing how in Nature, which is not always so wonderful after all, is full of things that live for the single purpose of sucking the gore out of your veins and gobbling your goddamn hemoglobin...

Paradise.

Well, it is pretty nice, actually, if you can overlook the fact that hot weather plays Ma and Pa to a great many life forms that you won't often run into in places like Omsk or Reykjavik For one thing, there are countless snails (the Brits call them "slugs"). They live in curlicue little shells of a design that a clever souvenir-seller could transform into earrings or decorations for sandals. They like moisture and attach themselves to walls, doors, and gates. Apparently, they are very good for your skin if you have the stomach to attach them to you, as the bodies that emerge from their shells are long, clammy (even meaty in a bizarre sort of way), graceful, and full of protein.

Frogs abound as well. They will come and sit on the patio, paying no heed to the curious dogs. I am fond of them. I am a friend to all forms of life that do not try to suck my blood. Meanwhile, the owls have come back and resumed their places in the belfry of the house opposite. On my balcony, the birds chatter and scream from the first hours of the morning, and in the distance comes the tenor monotony of the cuckoo, as regular as a clock.

When the dogs and I emerge from the jungle-path, we climb the bald and broken path up into the hills, sometimes seeing a large, big-eared rabbit who, becoming aware of me and my canine friends, bounds lithely away, sometimes with Pop and Cass in avid but fruitless pursuit. For them, the chase is enough. They are not hunters. They have never caught anything and probably they never will. But they never cease trying. Overhead, a black crow or an eagle will glide and swoop from time to time, ever watchful, and it makes me aware of Nature as a savage banquet, a wilderness-restaurant that is always open, especially at night. Lizards with gorgeous designs - green and purple - slither in the grass, and sometimes a snake will be found sunning itself out on the path.

This is a megalopolis of a different kind. It is a city not of millions but of billions.

Walking along the paths, one finds mosque after mosque that house the industrious, ever-artful ants. These oval edifices represent the craft of skillful engineers and a workforce beyond counting. The ants are as clever as the ancient Romans in that they build according to a plan that is repeated over and over, and so their grand houses are always circular and resemble a plethora of little coliseums. Sometimes these sand-castles get crushed, and then the ants build them again. Now and then a hard rain will drench them, but the ants persist. They never slack off, and I never bother them. I respect their homes enough to walk around them. Why destroy something for no reason?

So this, then, is a city of a different kind. One hears the blare of birds and not of car horns. Limpid summer flocks that grace the skies like airborne ballerinas - those are the pretty ones, like the springtime girls in big city parks. The sobs of the nocturnal dogs like lonely people in huge apartment complexes. The watchful predators, the blood-suckers - just like in a city of humans.

There but for fortune go the dogs and me - just at the edge of it all, little more involved than the tiny tinted bullets full of people so often mutely floating overhead, leaving trails of alabaster gas. Poppy loves the dark wood, but huge gentle Casper would be no match for it. He has grown too civilized; if abandoned to the forest his would become a bewildered soul. The very idea of his fear, his helplessness, touches me deeply, for even in the wake of contentious old age, I have saved up a storehouse of mercy like vats of honey. And once in a while - like the other night when there was a tremendous electric storm which my wife and I and our 'children' watched together from the bedroom balcony - I am gifted by hearing nature cry out in full throat as it preaches its thunderous sermon. Then comes lightning: the great x-ray machine that makes a sudden ballroom of the sky and then blots out all chandeliers.

Coming back home, the dogs and I pass between houses. Behind one, yet another hog is being groomed for the slaughter, and the smell of its piled dung is overwhelming - but in a 'country,' not human, way. Across from it there is a vicious-sounding canine who always snarls at us. But suddenly I see four new puppies in its wake. Life is always happening. So I speak gently to the big black and white mother who responds by growling and snarling with renewed force. I guess she will never be my friend.

And then one encounters the human neighbors behind fences or standing near their gates. They either smile or stare. Some talk, friendly-like, but I think you don't really ever get to know such people.

Gradually, I am finding out things about villages, just as I learned to know about cities. In the urban smog, the people are known by light from their phones. In the village, many of the older one look like piles of small stones and the children like feral cats.

I go home. There have been many 'homes', but this one may be the last. As I look out the window over the field, I see a grand, weedy overgrown bowl, splashed with the red hue of many poppies surrounded on all sides by the offspring of spring and its green collisions. I listen to the wind that courses through the now-full crowns of the trees.

Out there in that emerald megapolis that leads to the sea, minute by minute, there is birth, death, and Armageddon. All played out under a reptilian sun. No love at all. Only the florid images from which love is imagined and seizes energy.

I guess this afternoon, I will grab a shovel and go take care of that dead forest dog.

I don't want the poor fellow to be left there in rotting paralysis among the other still living things. Seems to me that amid the terrible onrush of all this savage, paradisiacal beauty, and even among the garbage strewn by the human engines, there ought to be a little dignity too. I guess the brief urge to be merciful is one thing we humans can, on occasion, muster.

A CATCHER IN THE RYE

Sometimes when I go walking with my dogs in Bliznatsi, Bulgaria, early in the morning, we take a certain route up toward the mountain forest, past fields of still-glistening mud from recent rain and melted snow, and emerge onto a path near one of the many summits; this one seems to diverge in all directions - and, of course, all roads hint at all possibilities.

For a second or two, I have the same sensation each time. I feel as though I am Alexander the Great (or some such 'superman' of the distant past), standing there trying to decide where to go and who to conquer next. Just a momentary self-flattering myth and nothing more, and yet maybe I am not remiss in imagining that such visions were actually what those implacable marauders of bygone ages experienced in their own minds.

The vision is helped by the fact that nobody else is around at such an early hour (6:00), and I have the mountain all to myself - if you discount the myriad little creatures that string the earth together underfoot and the early adventurer-birds that dance in the trees or make boomeranging formations in the sky. The dawn seems like a vast egg that has been cracked open, spilling out its yolk amid the reddening squawk of many farm-land roosters.

In these brief intervals when there are absolutely no problems to be solved, and no one to quarrel with, be annoyed by, or hate - I feel ageless. All the frustrated animosity of the years dissipates, and the dreamworld returns, the fantasies unbroken, and my nostalgia for things that never were somehow reassembles the lost ghosts, while the breeze seems a faintly audible orchestra playing on some distant village green in a rustic town that never was. Amid this rebirth, I am as Alexander surveying the world, but I feel no need to 'conquer' anybody.

One of the things that happens to you when you start to get old is that you begin, not merely to relive the past, but to tinker with it.

I guess part of the idea is to try and figure out where you got it right and where you blew it, messed it up, and sent it all to hell. And fix that part, if you can. Not by changing it (there are no time machines) but by revising your conclusions. Moreover, given the absolute fact that long-term memory survives the years whereas short-term memory can't recall the lunch menu, I find myself engaging in these utterly futile conversations that I had with people (usually women) years and years ago. I can remember (or so I imagine) what was said almost word-for-word, the only difference being that now I know what I SHOULD have said. And so I say it.

Thus, with a graying heart and brain, I find myself wondering if my whole life would have changed (and of course the fate of the world) if I had just said "this" instead of "that". I wonder. And then I remember that those people (women) told me goodbye fifty years ago. It reminds me of a little dialogue I read once, where a small boy was walking with his grandmother in a cemetery some forty years or so after the end of the American Civil War.

"Why did they have to die?" the little boy asks the grandmother (who remembers those days). She pauses for a minute, then replies "Well, they'd all be dead by now anyway." I don't know why, but it struck me that those would be exactly the words that many melancholy, but rigid, old women, their men long-gone in the meaningless wars, might say to such a question.

I look at my two great dogs, and it occurs to me, as they wag their tails and glance back at me from time to time, that for them the world is a wonderful place. I want them to always think that. Our first dog, Poppendoshka, simply appeared at our door one morning in Moscow seven years ago. She had been abandoned in the dead of winter, and I will never know how she got into the building. Or came all the way upstairs to the top floor, sitting there waiting- to the complete astonishment of my wife Liuba and me - when I opened the door to go to work. Maybe there is a God after all.

Casper, the powerful stream-lined Rhodesian ridgeback retriever, came later. Poppy is feisty, Casper totally gentle. Cass was born with his testicles locked inside him and needed an operation. Then he was fine. Anyway, both of them share the belief that the world is a good place, and I encourage them in that assessment. So I, who am mostly without faith, nevertheless, try to feed faith in those who still feel it. It seems like the right thing to do.

It puts me in mind of when I came face-to-face with a deer in a forest back in North Carolina. We startled each other, then stood and looked into each other's eyes. Finally, the deer trotted off, that gorgeous, golden body rippling as it went. It made me wonder how anyone could possibly wish to kill such an animal and call it 'sport.' But they do, and at such times I feel like an alien on this planet.

As we walk down the hill toward home and breakfast, here, even in Bliznatsi, one encounters the inevitable monuments and markings of human waste. Beer bottles, plastic water containers, abandoned shoes, rotten tires from who knows what cars or trucks, rags, cigarette butts and wrappers - the stench of human experience. Undaunted, the simple dogs, beneath the simple flocks of birds, next to the simple saplings that soon will be full-bearded and wild-haired like pagan men and women in the heat of summer, back when the world was younger -- go panting by, Casper's healthy bollocks jostling in all freedom as he bounds along on his beautiful, lithe, mahogany legs.

I want to protect those dogs from evil. I want them to live and die believing that the world is a kind of heaven. And in this way I remember J.D. Salinger's famous book, in which Holden Caulfield, the rebellious hero, has this vision of himself standing at the edge of a cliff where children are playing in a field of deep rye. The children are innocent and unknowing, and sometimes in their frolics they steer too close to the edge. It is the job of the 'Catcher', there to protect them, to grab them and pull them back when they teeter too near the brink.

He is The Catcher in the Rye.

That's me with my dogs as we pass through the garbage that offends even such a placid, sun-sprinkled, and heaven-blessed place such as the one I'm in. It is like a field of dead soldiers and I, like that old woman, try to explain things to my dogs that in fact I know nothing about. And I tell them, paraphrasing Caesar in my typically obscene manner, "Dogs, I saw, I conquered, I came."

They wag their tails.

I am here to save them from the abyss as best I can, to keep them from getting loose and straying into the roads where sour-breathed oblivion coils and lurks in wait, with flicking tongue or jaws dripping with anticipation. Long corrupted and rotting with age, I strive to be their angel.

2.

SAY-HEY DAYS

CANNED LAUGHTER

When I was a kid back in America, there were these sit-coms on TV. I must not have had much to do, because I watched them. *I Love Lucy. Make Room for Daddy. Leave it to Beaver.* And a bunch of others. In those days there were westerns in the evenings, but because of political correctness or maybe just changing tastes, they don't make them anymore. The comedies were all good, clean 1950s fun, but what always struck me was the way, when someone told a joke, a volley of laughter would erupt from the 'audience.' Except that I knew there was no audience, and, furthermore, not all of it was that funny. So who in the hell was doing all the laughing? Moreover, it sounded mechanical and... disembodied... like something someone kept rewinding with a handle again and again at signaled intervals which nowadays we would describe as algorithms or bots...

I do understand a basic principle of laughter that states that all it takes is for one person to start chuckling and giggling and then others will follow. Like yawning. Or standing in the middle of the street gazing up at the sky. The domino effect. A very antisocial friend of mine once described how he would do precisely this, and then after curious passers-by joined him in his heavenly scan - looking for God or some guy on a rooftop about to jump off and commit suicide - he would just walk away.

I've heard there is even a form of psychological treatment known as 'laughter therapy.' Apparently, depressed people get together (with the aid of a trained psychologist) and somebody just starts guffawing like an inmate in Bedlam. Har har, ho ho, hee hee. I don't know but I would guess that an awkward moment of silence from the others ensues, and then, slowly, hesitantly, then more resolutely, and finally, all restraint hurled to the shadows like the totally spontaneous gyrations of a train which has just jumped the tracks, the avalanche begins: "Yuck, yuck, hahaha, axaxax, yo ho ho, moo haw haw" - one answering the other with the same brewing undertow of panic of lambs baa-ing on a hillside when the wolf has been spotted, and before you know it, the whole house is splitting its sides, phlegm and spit flying everywhere as the jubilant subjects chortle and cackle and piss themselves in a fruitless effort at regaining self-control. After that, they are healed of their depression. Or such is the directive.

For a while in Moscow a kind of street art called 'mob dancing' became the rave. I liked it. I have seen it at airports and lakes. Say you are at a big airport or urban station where there are a lot of people. Suddenly one person gets up and starts dancing and then another and another. Soon half the station is doing it and, quite frankly, I find the overall effect rather marvelous. Street art based on human traffic. A testimony to human energy and creativity and happiness. The same as with the lake I saw online where one person, fully dressed, walked into the lake and started gyrating around. Again, there was that pregnant pause, and then another went to the lake, and soon the lake was full. Fully dressed people, celebrating life in the water. Waving and rejoicing. And a gale ran through me; I felt, for a blink of time, orgasmicly connected to a cosmic unity.

The only trouble was that it was NOT spontaneous; it was entirely choreographed. Behind the scenes there had been event-organizers, maybe even practice sessions to get the timing down. This realization did not ruin it for me - I still thought the idea was pretty cool. And besides, as Shakespeare wrote long ago, "All the World's a Stage/and all the Men and Women merely Players." W.B. Yeats, much later, understood this as well and wrote, albeit with sadness behind the language: "Players and the painted stage took all my love/and not those things that they were emblems of." And so, though it sounds curmudgeonly to say so, the mob dancing was all fakery.

A great deal of life is a fake: pretending astonished delight upon opening a Christmas present whose contents you have been informed of in advance; behaving solemnly at a funeral when in fact you are glad the bastard is dead and hope that great pain accompanied his demise; the psychopathic killer who joins the search party and looks for the body that he himself has ditched somewhere in the next county; the husband who says I love you and the wife who says I love you - and neither means it.

And yet to declare it all fake and therefore dismiss it as nothing but hypocrisy signifying nothing - it's a bit too pat and smug, isn't it? Condescending, as if one stands imperiously above it all, totally immune to deceit and self-hoodwinkery. And this drives me to the question: Does it matter if it is fake as long as it works? And isn't much of life just a matter of going about our business, trying to maintain order, and not piss it all away (at least not all at once?) How many Kodak moments (as they used to say) can there be? How many authentic encounters with the eternal, when the sky rips apart for a split second and you see, you see, what is beyond your limitations - except in that moment - before the sky sews itself up shut again and restores the oppressive and overcast canopy?

Art, I have decided, is at its very best the attempt to capture the eternal in the ephemeral. Two of my favorite paintings, for example, are *The Girl with the Pearl Earring* and, yes, I confess, the *Mona Lisa*. Both have been so over-commercialized that one needs to debrief one's soul in order to gather renewed energy and simply gaze into the oils of the women, as if for the first time. But i can do it. And what haunts me is not only the fabled expressions in the women's eyes, and on their lips and faces, but what I really ache to know: Who were they? And, more to the point, what were they up to in the minutes and hours before and after the artists finished their sessions? To see them from many different angles and even through the passing years. After all, both women were as real as people sitting in a train station or on a bus. They were somebody. But Who? What we see is only the contrivance, the assumed expression, the dazzling glimpse of the ephemeral...suggestive of the eternal. I cannot follow Lisa Gherardini home. Thus, it is impossible ever to be disappointed by her.

Yeats wonders, "How can we know the dancer from the dance?" -- and I, less eloquently of course, have asked myself the same question. And it used to matter more than it does now. I used to lie in bed and listen to music on the radio, and sometimes behind the main vocalist you could hear the voices of women singing the choruses. I always wondered who they were and where they went. In small towns, as a little boy, I didn't look at the shops so much as at the windows above them. I would wonder what went on up there. And many years later in Moscow, I would be standing out on my balcony and smoke and gaze at the vast checkerboard of windows of the building opposite, trying to imagine the lives going on in there: laughter, sex, hard work, alcoholism, dreams, brutality. The windows told me nothing and everything.

When I used to go to job interviews back in America, I was informed that I had to 'sell myself.' And indeed, I have witnessed with my own eyes over these many years that Appearance often counts for more than Reality, the Surface more than Depth, and Style over Substance. I seriously doubt that it has ever been any different with the human race in any age. Different day, same shit, as my Russian journalist friend Dmitri says everytime I ask him how's it going?

And yet, sooner or later, we are found out, aren't we? - and I think that the trick is to live as if at any moment you might happen to be seen, like a veil being lifted from a statue, you would not embarrass yourself too much. And that what was faked and what was real were not oceans or galaxies apart.

My grandmother told me, there in front of our old black and white TV, that most of that canned laughter had been recorded years previously and that some of that chorus, howling with mirth, were probably dead and turned to stone. We both laughed at that one, and for years I had a vision of dead bodies cackling all the way from their coffins right into the TV studios.

Maybe I am wrong, but I think it says a lot about life, when one accepts that it's mostly choreography punctuated sometimes by kisses of real passion, and genuine sobbing when a loved one dies. We live in the ephemeral, but we cannot escape the eternal. Whoever Vermeer's girl was, whoever la Gioconda was - and whatever they thought about, they were real people, and if we had known them, we would have liked some things about them and disliked others. And we would ALWAYS have been deceived!! What I know is that seeing their portraits makes me happy; understanding that I cannot touch them makes me sad.

It's like happiness and the fact that most people in affluent countries keep asking themselves "Am I happy? Am I happy? Am I happy?"

Then, much later, as we walk along on windy autumn streets, watching young people on their evening promenades wearing the bright, tight sweaters and thigh-hugging jeans that are preludes to the naked warmth and sexual writhing they will soon share in rooms now beyond us, we will say: We wore those uniforms once ourselves; we say: Yes, that was happiness. That was when we had it. And it seemed real.

THE SLEEK, BLEAK UTTERNESS OF MAKE BELIEVE

It was during the otherwise unchallenged years of my boyhood that I started to understand my limits, and it started with my indoctrination into Little League Baseball. You see, like Martin Luther King in the 1960's, my grandfather also had a dream. And that dream was that I would become an outstanding baseball player, maybe even a Major Leaguer.

He fed me this dream and tried his best to sell me on it. He also imagined that I could and would star in basketball, which apparently had been his best sport long ago. Being still afire with his own unrealized opportunities and potential, he determined, most innocently I believe, that I should succeed where he had…not failed so much as had been denied. Cheated even. In his thumping West Virginia heart and his windy mind - battered by bleating winds atop many telephone poles - he made up his mind that, whereas he had been robbed of his chances, I would be pushed forward. By him. I could be a champion.

He thought that a skinny boy with a jerking head and facial tic, ashamed of his nervous hands and narrow, stupid little feet, hummingbird bones, and Tweety-pie adolescent dick could be the next Jerry West. (Michael Jordan and LeBron James were still a long way off, and, besides, I doubt that even Grandpa's obsessive will could have changed the color of my skin.)

The terrifying old heavyweight boxing champ Sonny Liston once said of former champ Floyd Patterson, whom he twice demolished in one round, "How do you tell a bird he can't fly?" And my grandfather was as wrong as Floyd Patterson ever was. But I spent my adolescence and early teenage years trying to be what he wanted. The failure of that project commingled with the indifference of the girls and a cold shoulder from the 'cool' guys I wanted to buddy-up with left me feeling like a gloomy little leftover snowball in a Vivaldi springtime, and made me start despising the human race.

That remembered sense of disaffection has never gone away, and it's a damn good thing that I have always had a poet's crazy love of life inside me plus an overriding capacity for gentle feelings; otherwise, I might be famous only for exterminating people at some huge public gathering. It is because…out of such frustration, thwarted goals, and inability to fit in, that the most malevolent unchained rage is sometimes born.

If baseball hadn't fastened itself, anchor-like, to a required protocol in the summer, I might have been able to spend more time with Mom over in Martinsburg, but when the season approached there was no question of focusing on anything else. And to be truthful, I wanted it too. It's not like Grandpa threatened to lock me in the trunk of the car if I refused to play. I was just as eager as he was. Our team was sponsored by Big Star Supermarket, and so we were called "Big Star" (what else?) We wore green uniforms and played against teams with names like "Humphrey's Church', "The Diamond (the biggest department store in Charleston), 'The Odd Fellows' (sounds gay, doesn't it? But in fact this was the name of some big social club in town), and 'The Marines' — always the dominant team, whose manager was a Major League prototype 'skipper' with the illustrious name Kermit Kaiser. His team was a local legend.

We played at Bigley Field, a spread of ball-playing real estate which, like the vacant lot where Jimmy Brumbaugh and I lived out our epics, looked massive then but probably would have shrunk a lot by now, if I ever saw it again. It had been cultivated and manicured into a tidy little ball diamond, and for me this precise baseball geometry has always represented one of life's perfect forms, whether in sunshine or under floodlights.

Beyond the outfield fence there was a huge softball park extending way over to another set of bleachers and the street beyond, and games were always going on over there too. Those were adult leagues, slow pitch and fast pitch, and I loved to walk over and watch them when I had time. The field had lights and we played twice a week. Sometimes we went first and sometimes we had the second game. I loved playing 'under the lights' - it really felt like the Big Leagues. It felt like playing inside some sort of dream.

I had this dreamlike feeling when I was in bed at night. I had a radio in my room, and I would turn it on as low and quiet as possible and listen to broadcasts of the Cincinnati Reds. My Granny, the one who was always trying to commandeer my insomnia and force me to go to sleep, must have had a sneaky kind of mischievous wisdom in her soul, because it just occurred to me (five minutes ago, to be exact) that she could have removed that radio any time she wanted. But she didn't. If I heard her coming up the brown staircase with its odd little creaks and sighs, I would shut it off at once and dive headlong into my I-am-asleep mode.

Those ball games, which I started listening to after we moved from the flat, paneled house on Woodbine Avenue down to the white, ramshackle four-story job (if you count basement and attic) on the dead-end road at the bottom of a bending slope called Carson Street, were a lifeline to heaven for me. A night-heaven made of things glowing sharply amid ever-evolving shadows. And those specters ran around the green fields that existed somewhere in that radio box. I would listen to Waite Hoyt, the old Ruthian Yankee ace from the 1920s and his sidekick Joe Nuxhall, a lefty hurler of brief fame with the Reds, describe the action, and I would feel, there in the darkness, a tremendous sense of security, as if Waite and Joe were assuring me that everything was okay. I guess I felt the great glories of the womb all over again, the storms of creation, and heard the thundering bats of Ruth and Gehrig when I heard Waite and Joe tell me about the game they were watching, their voices coming from out of the inside of that little white box.

It wasn't Philadelphia or Los Angeles those games were coming from, but from some special sanctuary that I craved the protection of, and I had no conception whatsoever that maybe after the game Waite and Joe would leave the broadcast booth, loosen up with a round or five of drinks and maybe chase a couple of blondes - No ! I couldn't have conceived of it, and that was not owing to any moral judgment of things - because, most definitely I have few morals in the conventional sense - but it was from a wider disbelief, a plaster-eyed non-recognition of the fact that Waite and Joe and all those Cincinnati players were real people. To me, they existed merely to climb into that box every evening and stay there until the last out; that is, they were stimulants to my ungovernable imagination. Otherwise, how could they really exist, except as like mannequins in a department store display, mere voices in the deep theater of my mind. I loved nothing more - nor had ever felt so secure - than when it was only the third inning, with many innings left to go; but came the ninth of a not-close game, and I could feel a kind of anxiety creeping into me. I wanted those games to last forever the same way dying folks look for signs and glimpses of a new birth. The end of the game meant that the radio became just a box again, its magic strength gone like Sampson losing his hair. I wanted extra innings, or maybe even a long rain delay where they had nothing to do but talk; I just wanted Waite and Joe to talk away in that box, just keep talking the night away.

During football and basketball seasons Grandpa and I would listen to the West Virginia University games on the radio. This was long before cable TV and ESPN. We just had a black and white television, and back in those days you were able to see one college football game on Saturday and one pro game on Sunday, although at least with the pros, you had a choice because the Cleveland Browns were always on one channel and somebody from the other division on another one. I hated the Browns (being a New York Giants fan), but they did have a strong team featuring one of the greatest players of all time, Jim Brown. There were no doubleheaders and no night games televised in football, although on Sunday afternoons you could sometimes watch the Redlegs play two games, like they did in those days. No Monday Night Football.

The Mountaineers of West Virginia University were lousy at football most of the time (we listened to the games anyway), but the basketball team was another matter. In the days before I had come of age enough to be interested in what was going on, a crazy guy called Hot Rod Hundley had played for the 'Gold and Blue.' Hundley, of course, was a white man because the race barrier was still in force; not many teams had black players, and if they did, they were the star players. Otherwise, they were not welcome. So there were no 'coloreds' cluttering up the bench. In the Deep South, segregation as a way of life was hanging on for dear life, and there were no black players at all for the simple reason that there were no black students. Places such as the University of Alabama, the University of Mississippi, etc., were Lily White. It wasn't until JFK, ML King and the Civil Rights Movement arrived and gathered steam that all that began to change.

Nevertheless, the all-black Harlem Globetrotters were popular - as a curiosity piece (at an earlier time they had competed for real) - and they specialized in a lot of show-boating and tricky ball-handling which pleased the crowd to no end. Guys with interesting (and suggestive) names like 'Sweet Water Clifton' played for them, and for years their Entertainer-in-Chief was a comedian called Meadowlark Lemon. They barnstormed around all over the country and the world and, now that I consider it (as I write this morning), nothing could possibly have been more indicative of the incredible double standard that existed back then. Those black men, as I see it now, were viewed in the same light as circus animals. White people loved them. Loved them the same way they loved ponies and elephants under the Big Top. They could do tricks and shake their manes and wag their tails, even roll over on their backs for treats, but never sit down at the same table for dinner.

Anyway, Hundley - sort of like Elvis Presley would soon do - had learned some magic and borrowed some antics from the Trotters. He was a great player and compulsive showman, and during Mountaineer games he would put on the razzle-dazzle.

Opponents would go through the roof, moralistic newsmen would pen diatribes about his disgraceful monkey shines on the court - and the crowds LOVED it. Hod Rod went on to a moderately successful pro career and later became one of the best broadcasters in the business. A winner at life, it seems.

But the Real Deal for WVU basketball arrived in 1958 in the form of Jerry West. In the NFL, the New York Giants middle linebacker Sam Huff had played for the Mountaineers and he was a famous guy, but without question West was the greatest athlete ever to put on a Mountaineers uniform. So Grandpa and I, during basketball season, would religiously listen to the games as West Virginia became good enough to join the nation's elite. The announcer in the booth for those radioed-in games was a man named Jack Fleming who, to my way of thinking, had the most wonderful voice I had ever heard.

Deep in my heart I probably already knew (Grandpa didn't) that I would never amount to much as a ball player. So it became my ambition to follow in Jack Fleming's footsteps and become a sportscaster. But I needed a way to practice my new trade.

The answer came in the form of a tape recorder on one of those magnificent Christmases that I enjoyed as a boy - and an 'only child' at that. Back then, tape recorders were not small. Mine was a large contraption, as big as one of those old-fashioned Victrolas that you played records on (45s and 33s).

Whatever, it came straight from heaven. Right away, I decided to start broadcasting make believe football and basketball games. Even at that age, I was something of a genius at this sort of thing. I would study the rosters of the teams for the upcoming game, I would make an assessment of who the likely winner would be.

Then I would sequester myself in a distant room where Grandma's voice calling me to dinner wouldn't fuck up the realism I was striving for (Imagine being in the Press Box at Mountaineer Field and all of a sudden, during a tense moment in the action, you can hear Mrs. Fleming yelling "Jack, where the hell are you? Your baloney sandwich and chocolate milk are on the table !"). So I would hide and simply start: "Good afternoon, ladies and gentlemen! This is Jack Fleming welcoming you to Mountaineer Field in Morgantown where today the 1 and 5 Mountaineer squad will play host to the Fighting Illini of Illinois, whose record stands at 3 and 3. The weather is cold but clear and it should be a great day for a football game !" And so on. And I would sit there for two hours just making up the game as I went along, chattering away (WVU lost of course). It was the make-believe world that I felt totally comfortable in.

The only problem was when I heard my own voice for the first time. It's when I learned that we never sound like we think we do. I thought I was doing a perfect imitation of Jack Fleming. In fact, I had the high-pitched voice of an 11-year old girl who had just sat down on a thumb tack. I was so embarrassed that I almost gave up on the idea of being a sportscaster then and there.

I came up with another brilliant idea as I delved deeper into my own world, and I sometimes wonder now if people in the present day, especially the so-called 'Millennials', don't look for the same escape hatches and derive the same satisfaction from virtual reality and the gaming industry. I get the feeling that they just live for the moments when they can disappear into these phantom worlds, and I even sense that some of them would not mind if they never had to come back.

My idea was to play a whole season of baseball games with one club. Of course, I couldn't do the 154 game schedule as it was back then before the league added more teams and expanded the schedule to 162 games. So, being realistic, I settled on a 36 game schedule. The plan was to cut up many small strips of paper and on each one write something that could happen in a ball game, repeating those things that were sure to happen most frequently in the correct proportion that they would be sure to occur. For example, in any at-bat there is usually some sort of sequence such as Ball one, Strike one, Ball Two, Foul ball (Strike two),

Ground out. Or Strike one, Ball one, Ball Two, Ball Three, Hit by Pitch. Or Strike one, Single (or Double), I made provision for stolen bases and caught stealing, errors by infielders and outfielders, home runs, etc. By the end of this process, all possibilities had been accounted for. Naturally, it took a lot of experimenting because for me the pay-off wasn't to achieve some speeded-up pinball machine effect, but to approximate real-life as much as possible. That's probably where I was different from how most kids my age would have gone about it. To me, attention to detail was paramount.

When I decided I finally had it about right - and dumped all my data into an old Lincoln Logs container that I hadn't used in ages, the next thing to do was select a team. I was well aware that since everything was going to depend on chance, it would not be wise to choose either a top team or one at the absolute bottom. So that meant the Yankees were out because they were too good in real life. In my set-up, drawing game situations out of a hat (so to speak) would presumably produce a .500 ball club, and that would never do for the Yankees. Likewise, at the other end of the spectrum, so I knew I had to avoid fuck-heads like the Washington Senators and Kansas City Athletics. No, I had to choose a middle-of-the-pack ball club, maybe one a little bit worse than average, so even if they did better than expected it would be a surprise but not a travesty of my purposes. So I chose the perennially mediocre Chicago Cubs. Then, once everything was in order, I turned on the tape recorder: "Good afternoon ladies and gentlemen! This is Harry Caray welcoming you to Wrigley Field…" I played the whole 36-game season that way. I even kept statistics: batting averages, pitchers' earned run averages, the lot.

Maybe my most ingenious idea came just before the first Sonny Liston-Cassius Clay fight. We had a portable TV set, and if you turned the channel to anything but the three that were available, what you got was a fuzzy white screen that we called 'snow.' If you turned up the volume, there was this "Shhhhhhhh" sound, and you could make it as loud as you wanted. To my ears, it could be transformed into the sound of a crowd at a sports event, and if you turned it up and down quickly it sounded like the reaction of a full stadium to some guy scoring a touchdown or hitting a home run. I figure it would be perfect to simulate the excitement of Liston-Clay (I had Clay losing after putting up a great fight in the early rounds). In my opinion, it worked like a dream.

My last creative project toward the goal of sports self-appeasement was, of course, basketball. The dream (my grandfather's) was that I would make it as a player, but a little court time had already taught my head if not his heart that this was never going to happen. Yet since he had instilled a dream in me, a painful desire - and I had accepted it with open arms - I had to make it happen somehow, even in some psychological context that had nothing to do with reality. In short, I had to invent something that would work in my shadow world and compensate for my mediocrity in the harder, colder, fiercer world outside where my flimsy 'weapons' were not sharp enough to make me a 'winner'.

So I used to take a big soup tub (a saucepan, the English call it) and put it at the far end of my bed. This was after we had moved to Carson Street, another house up in the hills above Charleston. It was a big barn at the end of a dead-end street, as I have said. My bedroom was upstairs. I would roll up several socks tightly so that they were like a ball - unbounceable, but still a ball for my purposes, and then…what would I do?

I would dance about the bedroom, pretending to be two basketball teams - usually the Lakers and Celtics. I would flip about and drift and dart like players do on real courts - and otherwise pass the rolled-up sock (the ball) back and forth until I decided I was in a shooting position, and then I would let fly at the basket (the saucepan). The three-point shot hadn't come in yet, but I would often shoot from a distance just to make it more challenging. And of course, there were logistics problems that had to be surmounted and which, with me, took the form of hulking, arm-waving opponents.

So the encased light in the middle of the room became a defender's hand in my face; likewise, the curved inlay of the ceiling which blocked my view at the perimeters became reasons to adjust my shot. The big center was there waiting for the ball, and so I would whip it in, and move - because in basketball you must always move…and so Wilt or Bill Russell would pivot, move to the hoop and put it up, or else fire it back out (the 24-second clock running down) to West or Sam Jones or John Havlicek, who would let fly at the last possible moment. A lot of drama, as you can see.

When I gave the ball to the centers, there was an immediate situational problem. Of course, they could just lay it in (they were standing above my bed) – but that would be too easy; it would spoil everything. Therefore, the tall centers: Chamberlain and Russell, had to be taken into account. To make their life more difficult and their shots at goal more challenging, I would twist my body in order to render them off-balance, and therefore they would miss as often as they would hit. Anyway, Chamberlain liked to take fade-away shots after a lot of faking and maneuvering, and that was just fine. If the ball hit the wall and rolled off the bed onto the floor, that meant a foul had been committed and it meant two free throws were in order. (I had a designated foul line, naturally). That's how I kept the big centers towering over my bed honest. They couldn't just dunk - at least not until the end of those rare games that didn't come down to the wire. Then they could show off.

Grandma would scream at me if I made too much noise because her kitchen was just below, and in fact I am surprised that I didn't come crashing through the ceiling straight into the dull hamburger patties and pot of instant mashed potatoes (a recent miracle of mass production at the time) – but you know how it gets at the end of a tense game. One must grind it out.

Consciously or unconsciously (I think consciously) I would make sure the games were close and that it came down to the last shot. There would be one final time out. Then I would pass the ball back and forth, patiently. You may wonder how I knew the time? Well, that is simple. I had a clock with a second hand from a board game I had been bought at Christmas. With that wound-up clock, its second hand ever moving, I could keep time for quarters (pros) and halves (college) and most certainly control the last precious seconds of an NBA or NCAA championship game. I lived for those moments. Grandma could scream all she wanted. When I made that shot...it was like shooting your load into the mouth of the Nocturnal Emissions Maiden. Such is the life of the man/boy who must live on his dreams alone, without ever being able to win on the streets.

My other great success of imagination was down in the basement (I think every house should have one). I simply nailed some small, thin strips of wood together and made a little 'basket' that was correctly in proportion with a tennis ball. Then I nailed it to an overhanging rafter, which created a natural 'backboard'. There was plenty of space I could run up and down, back and forth, in, and of course that became the 'court.' So, as with the rolled-up sock in the upper bedroom, the tennis ball (which I could actually bounce - big engineering improvement) became the 'basketball.' and thus I played the games. I chose the University of Michigan that winter. That was when Cazzie Russell and Bill Buntin played for the Wolverines, and for some reason I chose them. As always, I used a clock, which I would wind up again during 'time outs'. Michigan, as in real life, usually won — and to accomplish this I probably created easier shots for them and more difficult ones for their opponents, but it all worked out in a way that approximated real life.

As I stated earlier, it was not so much otherworldly fantasy I was interested in as an approximation of reality - but a reality I could control. When I talk to young people today, what with their cyberspace adventures and increasingly elaborate video games - I get the feeling that they are more interested in rejecting the real world and substituting a fantastical fake or 'virtual' one in its place. I was only interested in the duplication of a perceived reality.

Where we are similar, I suppose, is that we all want to control the place we have created. They want to live in their make believe wonderland, and I wanted to live in an every-day-world whose 'reality' resembled down to the last detail the blocks and bricks, the comings and goings of the streets and avenues, ball courts and diamonds, everything that existed in front of or beyond my house. It's just that I desired and, desperately needed, it seems, to refashion this world, transform it so that I could be one of its heroes.

But I had no desire to remain Eric Le Roy in such a hallowed place of last second, championship determining twenty-foot buzzer-beaters. I wanted to forget Eric Le Roy and become Jerry West. It was as though I felt, deep inside of me, that Eric Le Roy was an invisible boy, something that God should have thought better of. Eric Le Roy was one of Michelangelo's discarded and forgotten sketches; Jerry West was the very statue of David.

It is the goal of all of us, I believe, somehow to be in absolute control of our environment. I have no idea what they did in the prehistoric, ancient, or medieval world. But in the modern world we, more and more, manufacture other, different realities when we don't like - and most of us don't - the realities we get stuck with. In many ways, I feel, it's the same with drunks and drug addicts. They (we) want to escape. And as I found out later, alcohol has the power to turn an Eric Le Roy into a Jerry West. Even if only for a few hours, one imagines oneself as the hero of his own life.

And in some cases, Jekyll becomes Hyde. It is my conviction that however much we try to adapt to - and pretend to enjoy - being Dr. Jekyll, most of us fantasize (some more than others) what it would feel like to be Mr. Hyde. He is the delicious dark one, the shadow-man, sensuous, evil, and he sneers at all limitations. I found this out many years later when I became addicted to crack cocaine.

I would get in the car in St. Augustine, often fit from the gym and ruddy with health, but with the compulsive plan of going to Jacksonville to one of the whore-and-crack houses where an overspill of the drug was always handy. It would be the ultimate sordid, wickedly jaded and brain-blowing ecstasy.

I knew a little Puerto Rican girl in one of those slum-houses who was known as Pony. She seemed able to produce one orgasm after the other when she was high. We would spend hours together and all she wanted in terms of payment was to hit the pipe - the glass stem, that is. So I would pick up some beer (tallboys) from the convenience store and start drinking them during the 50-odd minute drive to the ghetto. After about the second one, the alcohol effect would kick in, my mood would intensify, and I would start to visualize a handful of rocks, a pipe, and Pony.

The anticipation was always tremendous, and I remember the way I would look up at the rear-vision mirror and watch with interest how my face gradually started to transform from that of a clean-cut, rather nice-looking ordinary young man into the trashy, leering, almost devilish countenance of a greedy hobo.

THE IRON NECKLACE OF ORDINARINESS

There is an old picture of me that I will never see again. That's because it got lost in a suitcase that disappeared shortly before I left the United States for the last time in 2008. But it sits on a table in my mind along with a spangled deep purple music box I bought my mother when I was 8 years old and which played "The Anniversary Waltz" when you wound it up. Fast at first, then slower and slower until, like breath, it stopped.

I must have been around 16 years old in this photo, and in it I am wearing a plain black suit with a white shirt and thin dark necktie, and I am cradling a classic guitar. It is the guitar which sets the snapshot apart from any other that might have been taken of me at that age. Needless to say I am clean-shaven, my hair is parted on one side, the wider section barely descending in the direction of the brow over my left eye. I guess I have the pale, studious, perhaps Eastern European - maybe Hungarian or Polish (or do I flatter myself?) - aspect of a serious candidate at some solemn conservatory where frivolity and idleness are unknown.

A passport photo, in other words. But for the guitar.

At that period in my life, I practiced classical guitar no less than four hours every day. I had started out by being caught up in the folk music craze of the 60's, and my idols were Bob Dylan and Peter, Paul, and Mary. Problem was I couldn't sing. Forget Peter Yarrow, I couldn't even reach the level of Dylan's obnoxious whine. I was too shy to sing in public; when I tried, my voice either quavered and broke or sounded like stale air whooshing out of a flat tire, and people bowed their heads in embarrassment. Maybe to say prayers.

So, I fell in love with the guitar itself. No one encouraged me except my instructor, and even he seemed amazed by the way I became obsessed with it. And so why did I?

It made me feel unique. In Charleston, West Virginia, a lot of people played guitars, but none, I soon discovered, could play the music of the great Andres Segovia. Nobody but me, that is. And so, I was one of a kind.

Not in sports, for example, where I stretched my very modest abilities to the limit in order please my grandfather and wound up feeling only frustrated and furious at my ineptitude.

Not with girls. I tried and was mostly passed over in favor of the more popular guys. I was just a typical West Virginia bumpkin. Okay, a good student. What else?

When my steel-stringed rhythm 'ax' had been exchanged for the broader classical model with its catgut strings that could be made to tremble and sigh and sob - and so express the things of my soul that I wanted to let out - I got busy in a world of my own.

The bathroom was the best place to play because the acoustics were better in there, and in my spare time I listened to recordings of such artists as the immortal Segovia and the English virtuoso Julian Bream. By then I could read the music: Albeniz, Scarlatti, Dowland, Bach, and many others who had written music either for the lute or guitar, or whose music had been transcribed accordingly.

Soon, through careful listening, meticulous copying, and my own sensibilities, I knew how to make the music sound like it was supposed to sound. It was, you see, more than simply playing the notes. It was more like making poetry. I knew, something in me simply *knew*, how it was supposed to be, how long to pause, and how much pressure to put on the plucked strings. I instinctively understood all that, and it was a gift - and before long I was giving recitals and pretty much stunning the people of Charleston with my precocious ability.

I felt special because I THOUGHT I was special. At least in Charleston, West Virginia. Finally, I went to study in

Washington D.C. with an old Greek man named Sophocles Papas, who at one time had actually been a student of Segovia's. It was a blistering summer in Washington. Not being able to sleep (I had a room at the YMCA, and - yes - there were homosexuals there, as rumored, and I was afraid of them), I would sit in the park - scorching even at midnight - or go to a coffee shop and read.

Alas, my last recital with Mr. Papas was something of a flop. Maybe I had worked too hard and hadn't had enough sleep. I was supposed to move my fingers flawlessly up and down the scales, and I kept fucking up.

"I expected better things from you," he said, but invited me back in a few months. And those were his last words to me because I never went back. In one of my strange turns of character, I just abruptly lost interest. Four hours a day for three years, and I simply said the hell with it. Ah, the loneliness of the long-distance runner! Once more ensconced in Charleston (I was a teenager, remember), my lifestyle changed completely. I started drinking, partying, and going after the girls, and I had decided that if I could no longer discipline myself to practice properly, I should give up the guitar. As if it had never existed.

I was 17 by then. I am now 70. I have never picked up a guitar since.

I did a lot of cool things: I traveled, I studied at university, and my other titanic creative interest - writing poems - eventually won me a Ph.D. (I composed a 'creative' doctoral dissertation at Florida State.) But no one at the university recognized my 'genius'; I was just one of many talented people in writing programs across America.

There were times when I scribbled with the same ardor and abandon, my head stuffed full of dreams, as when I used to play "Leyenda" or "Malaguena," but there were dark sides in me - somber phantoms and night trains - and I began to gravitate toward Hades while acting out a fluctuating travesty that involved compulsive training on the one hand (weightlifting, boxing, distance running) and binge drinking and drug abuse on the other. I would get in a mood and just wander off, drift around. (I think the Australians call it 'going walkabout.') I met up with some strange people and the next thing you know I had the law on my tail. The cops in St. Augustine, Florida, hated me especially because they, being mostly racist rednecks at heart, despised the white college boy fuck-up who sponged off his Mom and hung out in Black-Ass Crack Town.

Thus, the young protege of long dead Segovia (my spiritual mentor) spent more time in the drink tank of the county jail stroking his penis than the nylon strings of a classic guitar.

Dream deferred; vision vanished.

I am fine now; obviously I have lived to tell the tale. Nor did the innate ability to "make it sound like it's supposed to sound" die with my abandonment of the musical instrument itself. I never stopped being a writer, but probably the only reason for that was that I couldn't leave behind the Purgatorial Hell that my brain had become. So whereas a guitar could always be forgotten at a train station, my mind went with me wherever I rambled. And it's a good thing that it's stuck between my ears; otherwise, I'd have left that bitch, too, at some greyhound bus terminal a long time ago.

Sometimes today when I write meaningfully and with love - not a political rant, but something about the deeper experiences of my life - I get that same old indescribable feeling of grace, and I know that what I am doing is good. But occasionally I wonder what might have been if I had just kept playing the guitar.

And, in a broader sense, I wonder how many other people have let their dreams slip away - perhaps not so much in the extreme manner that I did, but rather just peter out. Or, even worse, how many sooner or later decide that if they can't be special, then why the hell do it at all? That was me to a T.

Most people, you see - and I am one of them - reach the point where they have to come to terms with the fact that no matter how good they thought they were and tried to be, someone else was always better. They/We don't want to believe it, we holler and shout, we make excuses, we rationalize, we talk about 'tomorrow' - but gradually our voices, our cries, and our lives right along with it, just die down and fade away.

We have been tamed. As J. Alfred Prufrock states, "I am no prophet - and here's no great matter; I have seen the moment of my greatness flicker/And I have seen the eternal Footman hold my coat, and snicker/And in short, I was afraid."

We thought we were special, we dreamed we could do something to leave our mark on the world, only to realize gradually that we didn't have 'what it takes', and when the golden moments, those precious little windows of glittering chance, like wild birds suddenly flashing through a field and bringing a volley of Light, flashed before our eyes, we were too slow, or too distracted, or too frightened…cowardly…to respond like a champion. We didn't have it in us.

So a lot of people - maybe most - just give up and end up 'going through the motions.' Moreover, the sanctuary offered by the 'herd' mentality kicks in. After all, even when people are very young and going through their so-called 'rebellious' stage, they are usually frantic for acceptance, and many will risk their lives if it means being assured of group approval.

This carries right on to the all-determining, all-deciding matter of receiving 'likes' for a Facebook post. Such sweating aspirants prosper or perish according to this. You want to fuck up their day? Just ignore their post. The reality is the unreality; they simply disappear into cyberspace like raindrops into a puddle. So, conformity is king.

But the radical side of human character can rear its head also!! And that is a very intense need to be different, to stand out from the crowd. I remember seeing a cartoon in a magazine once that showed a thousand little bugs all huddled together - each the exact duplicate of the others - except that one was grinning like a fool, dancing around, and, in the caption, shouting triumphantly, "I've just got to be ME!"

Surely, guys like Beethoven and Einstein accomplished this. Abraham Lincoln and Nelson Mandela. But so did Adolph Hitler and Josef Stalin, Ted Bundy and Jeffrey Dahmer, Mark Chapman and John Wilkes Booth.

Would you assassinate an emperor or pope in order to be famous? Would you lick an asshole on national TV? Some have, some would, and some WILL. Give them time.

But 99.9% of the earth's transient population come and go without registering a bleep on whatever cosmic machine is counting the beans as they pass by on the conveyor belt. This drives some people crazy (me too). It's getting worse for us all. The slow demise of religion (which had the effect of transferring people's attention from themselves to 'God'); the Social Networking mania which throbs and pulsates every day with common madmen and women racking their brains nonstop trying to figure out how they, too, can go 'viral'; and the sheer speed of existence which has in effect reduced Andy Warhol's 15 minutes of fame idea down to about 15 seconds - leads people to want more than anything else simply to be remembered for
something, anything.

They want to be the best. Or at least unique. Maybe not in the world, but at least in the neighborhood. In James Joyce's great book of short stories called "Dubliners," there is one entitled "Counterparts," and it is a very depressing tale of an office worker named Farrington who is humiliated by his boss for inefficient work and then insubordination, and who then, lacking money, goes to pawn his watch in order to get drunk.

He sees a woman he finds attractive, but she ignores him. His rage begins to deepen. Finally, he ends up in a bar being challenged to an arm-wrestling contest by a younger fellow. Farrington, his cherished reputation as a strongman on the line, proceeds to lose twice. And this proves to be the crusher - his loss of the only real status he had. So he goes home and beats his children. That's how the story ends - with the pathetic kids promising to say Hail Mary's on his behalf if he will just stop hitting them.

The story is perhaps more complicated than my brief summary would allow, but what I have always been struck by in it is that Farrington's self-esteem manages to hold together until he is bested in the one area where he thought himself special, even impregnable. His self-image, based ultimately on that one claim to fame, is rent in ruins. It seems to me that many fragile people are able to keep their chin up because they believe themselves unique in at least one area. When I was at the University of Bath in England, there was a young guy, a student, who made it a point to never wear shoes. Never, not even on the coldest, rainiest days of the year. (And in England it rains a lot.) That was his 'proposition' - his way of saying, Look at me, World. I'm Standing Barefoot on the North Pole.

And I guess it worked. Forty-five years later, I don't remember his face, but I still remember seeing him walking around like that. Whatever he was trying to demonstrate or prove has elapsed away with him, along with the years. Yet a dim, tarnished, but still active image of his pale, common, unremarkable feet remains - like legend - and that's all.

Just for the hell of it, I checked the Guinness Book of Records, to find the nuttiest things people have done in order to be the best at something: They include a man who spent 16 years typing out the numbers from 1 to one million; a woman who set the record for speed in making a bed from bare mattress to finish: fitted sheet, top sheet, two pillow cases, fully buttoned duvet, and bed runner in just 74 seconds; the world loudest scream at 129 decibels; the guy who absorbed the hardest kick in the nuts (groin) ever recorded (there were others?) at 122 mph from an MMA expert; the man who blew out five candles with his own farts; the man with the longest beard (seven feet and eight inches); the guy who had 46 toilet seats broken over his head; and the guy who owned the heaviest working yo-yo (4,620 lbs.). Then there was the man with the tallest mohawk haircut (3 ft 8 inches) and the man (the only one I could envy) with the world's longest tongue (3.7 inches). Such a tongue I could put to good use.

It's a funny world, for sure, though I guess it depends on what you mean by funny. I remember working for a while in London as a door-to-door salesman. Colliers Encyclopedias. I remember trampling through the streets of the damp, misty, smoky London evenings among the brown council estates, watching as door after door opened briefly for me and then closed. I recall the countless pallid, cadaverous faces that appeared and disappeared like little ghosts, and (as I was still in my 20's) I remember imagining that I was patrolling a kind of makeshift death row, a very long one, and thinking, "All those people…whose lives do not matter. Where do they go?"

I guess Paul McCartney wondered the same thing in that song "Eleanor Rigby."

I have walked in huge cities, jammed into crowded metro stations and sandwiched onto trains at rush hour - so desperately without the possibility of movement that it was scary, and asking myself once: "Is it possible that there is a God who actually loves all these fucking people?"

I decided that No, there wasn't, there couldn't be. And then I realized that I was one of those people.

I have never, I see it clearly, been the world's best at anything. I feel important to my wife, useful to my dogs and cats, meaningful to my friends, valuable to my students and business contacts, and perhaps, when lit up with beer, I am still the Hero of My Own Life.

When I die, people will soon forget that I ever lived. But lest you think I am depressed, let me inform you that I am not.

You see, THEY think I am going to snuff it like everyone else, and yet I have a hidden plan to fool them all. This is because my own passionate sense of soaring, skyrocketing existence makes it impossible for me to imagine oblivion overtaking me and pulling me, like rude gravity, into a hole in the ground. I try and try and still can't believe it. A world without Eric Le Roy? Perish the thought!

Please forgive me that small joke. In fact, I know that when I die the air will quickly and efficiently seal itself around the space I occupied and zip it up with a tight Good Riddance! Those who knew me will fend for themselves in better ways than they did when I was egotistically attempting to prove that I was indispensable to them.

The question thus becomes, and I include myself in the inquiry: have we lived correctly? Authentically? Or did we somehow manage to screw it up? We were never all that good and, in the end,, we were easily replaced, and, anyway, God usually acted too tired to listen when finally, belatedly, we called out to Him from whatever foxhole we had landed in. Cringing.

It's a hell of a fix to be in, don't you think?

I remember that photograph of a callow but dead-serious young fellow sitting there with his magic machine poised in the grip of his left arm and right hand, his taut, narrow fingers stretching like miniature long-necked swans, this boy seemingly on the verge of it all - the fabulous things to come, I mean.
The photograph merely waits for him to lower his eyes, to curl his young body over the immaculate instrument, place his nimble fingers deftly where they should go, and begin conjuring some

haunting melody, as from a music box, out into the ineffable acoustics of the art-rich air.

For the future stretches out before him like something evoked by the quivering chords on a guitar, or maybe on great piano keys, or even the celestial wail of a church pipe organ.

This is immortality. Because he knows that he will always be there, always remembered by the others until *they* die.

HOW MUCH HAIR DO YOU WANT IN YOUR SOUP?

I sometimes wonder if eventually we will arrive at a completely hairless civilization. I mean, think of all the cartoons and caricatures you've seen depicting the 'advanced' people of the future. Shrunken in body, their globular heads stand out like huge melons, which of course - like most melons - are completely bald. The idea is to suggest a vast intelligence throbbing inside the glimmering fruit.

Think of all the futuristic films you have seen. Not only are the evil geniuses who threaten Our Way Of Life usually bald but so are most of the little green men who turn up as aliens in dark country lanes when the moon is a raging and aggressive orange. Again, the shiny skulls bulge under pressure exerted by what can only be massive, swamp-like brains capable of concocting reams of evil and ending Life as We Know It.

In such films, of course, there is always a crew of slavering, grunting hirsute hulks on hand as classic head-breakers in the employment of whatever Lex Luther clone is running the show, but these heavies are just window dressing, thrashing about in their chains until their chrome-skull Boss unleashes them to wreak havoc on Good Christian people.
The moral of the story is that the brightest bulbs are literally just that: bright bare glaring bulbs. Interrogation room equipment. The brain of Big Brother.

And speaking of morals, it is also true that clippers and sharp scissors have a lot to say about what the drill-masters are thinking. Aside from barber shops on Elm Street, there is nowhere that facial and scalp hair (among men) disappears faster than in the military and in prisons (the one existing to fight evil and the other to punish it). Ask most American moms and dads if they would prefer their young adult sons to look like they just got out of the Marine corps (in the style of 'peeled onions', as my Grandpa liked to call them) with domes as smooth as billiard balls and cheeks and chins barren of everything but pustules of acne - or to gyrate about sporting wild Medusa-like swirls of forest wildness on their heads and biblical beards that plunge from their jaws like angry sermons from tall mountains - and the answer will be plain every time: "Son, here are the garden shears and a wet cloth. Bathroom to your right. The mirror's on the wall above the sink."

A cropped noggin means NO NONSENSE. The message is simple: Lots of hair signifies a rebellious, subversive, anarchistic attitude out of step with the elevator music of the corporation and the whistle of the factory; conversely, a paucity or total absence of hair sends the message of seriousness, sobriety, tunnel-vision focus, cleanliness, and, above all, a willingness to forfeit all individuality for the sake of the SQUAD. And
the NATION.

Another point of interest is that long hair (and here both men and women fall under the umbrella together) has long been seen as symbolic of unruly virility (guys) and boudoir sensuality (gals). It explains why the biblical Samson's enemies decided that the best way to fuck his brain was to cut his hair. It depleted him utterly. Thus, in a culture where the Dionysian bent of spirit and an unbridled lust for bone-jumping are celebrated as attributes, one's hair is given liberty to flow.

Accordingly, at least in the past, the hairier a man's chest was, the more of a spunk-spraying Marlboro Man he was considered to be. (Now we live in an androgynous Age where it's better for him to have a pallid little 'breast' the color and texture of thinly rolled pizza dough.) When the Goon Squads take over and Iron Authoritarianism holds sway - and human sexuality is identified as nothing more than a bunch of vile degenerates in the act Squirting Dirt - Sin must be squashed, abolished, vanquished - and at this point human hair is counted by the strand by censors with flashlights and measuring sticks and purifying bonfires to the side.

What I take from this is that ascetic frigidity and a daily grind of anal retention exercises are the marks of the Modern Militaristic State - while long hair remains the province of the Untamed Pagan Tribe, whose Jungian shadow is always lurking and waiting for the chance to jump out of the darkness and hurtle beast-like into our minds.

Or am I indulging in too much psychoanalysis of culture? Probably it's because I grew up in the 1960's where hair became much, much more than a matter of personal choice or trendy style. Now, it's not worth fighting over, and even back then, in England, Ireland, Scotland, and Wales (it wasn't called the UK then) of the 1960s and early 70s it was even trendy for professional footballers to grow their hair long. The famous/infamous Irish superstar and love machine George Best springs to mind. The Brits were just cool cats, what with the Beatles and Stones, etc. And none of them were fighting in Vietnam.

'Nam' defined the America of that era just as much as did the Civil Rights Movement. Maybe even more, although they were entwined in the sense that many young black men, denied their civil rights as American citizens, were nevertheless drafted into the army to fight in Asia. They were cannon fodder in the Fat White Man's War.

This was also the age of the hippies, and these hippies were well-known for their long hair. There weren't a lot of black hippies, but the Soul Brothers who were on the same track developed their own unique hairstyle, which was known as the "Afro." Some of them were quite spectacular. Lew Alcindor (the early version of Kareem Abdul Jabbar) and most of the big-time athletes, musicians, and other entertainers were Afro-ed to the nines. Angela Davis, the Black Panther beauty, had a smooth oval face with an ebony treetop overlooking it. All the sheep in New Zealand couldn't have produced that amount of wool, and if they had, it would have been the wrong color. It was, as they sometimes say even today, "a black thing."

In the spring of 1968, a 'counter-culture' rock musical hit the Broadway stage. It was called *Hair* and was a celebration of the Bohemian life-style and anti-war idealism of a generation of young Americans known as 'the counterculture.' I caught the show in Manhattan and afterwards danced on the stage with the cast. (They had invited the audience to join them.)

But why would they call a Broadway musical *Hair*? Well, this is where hair had become very political. In fact, back then you would not have heard the word "fashion" to describe any of it. Hair had become a much more serious issue - one that would set fathers against sons and create ruptures in families that probably, in some cases, have never healed.

What do I mean? This was the baby boomer era, and the kids eligible for the draft during the Nam period were precisely the offspring of a soldier who had fought in World War II. The veterans of the Armed Forces had returned from Europe and the Pacific as heroes. Rightly so. The Nazis and warlike Japanese (they really were like hard guys back then, not averse to suicide missions which entailed pile driving into the sides of American warships, had to be dealt with). And that was just for starters. (Imagine a POW camp under Japanese authority when the Emperor's life and dignity needed salvaging at all costs.) So, rather justifiably, after Pearl Harbor it was understood that the time for larking about as 'isolationists' had ended. Yes, it stretches the realms of credulity, but the Americans - who now have their red, white, and blue-gloved fingers firmly embedded in every pot and pie worldwide - at that point wanted nothing to do with another European war. But they had no choice. And afterwards, the survivors returned as heroes. If there is an argument to be made against that, I can't make it.

So, with WWII ended and the enemy put to rout, you had these heroes returning to ticker tape parades. Some were in wheelchairs, others were still looking for their missing arms and legs, but it didn't matter. America was as happy as Bugs Bunny munching a carrot. The still-intact heroes and their wives then produced sons (and daughters). Two-car garages. Vacuum cleaners that would keep a wife happier than three orgasms in the same time it took to clean lint from the carpet. Kids whose smiles turned the soap and toothpaste industries into sky-line changing facades.

But pretty soon the new menace of communism had to be fought. Along came Vietnam and these now fully grown sons started getting letters from Uncle Sam to report to the nearest draft board.

But the problem was that Vietnam was a dubious venture from the start and a hard sell to the American public. Then things just kept getting worse and worse. A lot of young fellows couldn't understand why they were being asked to go fight against little yellow people on rice paddies on the total opposite side of the globe who seemed to pose no threat whatsoever to American security. Moreover, the lid had blown off many aspects of staid, lukewarm, conservative American culture, changing the mental landscape completely. Kids were getting high. Getting naked.

OF COURSE, for most people nothing much seemed to change. It is useful to recognize that even during the most critical periods of revolution and socio-political upheaval, the people out in the boondocks just carry on as usual and hope it will all soon blow over. Revolutions are fought by tiny mobs steered by ambitious politicians with big plans for THEMSELVES.

All this 'storming of the Bastille' mumbo-jumbo is mostly overrated; the real power orchestrating the changes (in that case Jacobins and Girondists) are operating behind the scenes.

This was also true in America. The long-haired dissidents had no more real power than the 'progressives' of today, but just like the progressives they were a loud and persistent presence. As such, they were all over the evening news. Students were occupying administration buildings on university campuses and raising a lot of hell. For all of that, the Vietnam War went on and on, long after LBJ had passed the baton to Richard Nixon.

Thus, while the farm boys out in Nebraska and Iowa dutifully went off to war (along with a disproportionate number of black people and poor kids of all backgrounds), the educated elites said Fuck You to authority and all the old war films starring Lee Marvin and John Wayne. They were listening to Bob Dylan. And so they said, "Hell No, We Won't Go!"

But gritty old Daddy Warbucks, sitting in the kitchen with his peeled onion and can of Budweiser, didn't want to hear that. Not at all. And when he looked at his 'coward' of a shaggy-ass son, the first thing he saw was that Long God Damned Hair. It became the symbol of two generations of Americans fighting to the death ideologically. In their own home.

A mop of hair. That's why they called the famous Broadway musical *Hair*.

The other day I read a blog that a guy had written regarding women shaving or not shaving their armpit follicles. It's nice to know, I guess, that while the physical appearance of the trendiest young men and women in the West, especially in Europe, has started to produce a look-alike effect wherein telling the difference between them gets harder and harder (I think it kinda sucks but that is not what this essay is about), it is probably becoming easier to choose clothes and toys and names. So the genders are blending. But the hair issue still sets them apart and persists in making statements.

Hair length for guys seems to be mostly non-political, but for women this is not the case. Maybe we are undergoing a cultural metamorphosis in which the men are turning into soap sculpture (shaving their heads and legs, etc.) and the women are shearing in places where they used to keep a mane of hair (there are a lot of cropped-headed women now) and in the pubic area (once referred to as their 'beaver'). Meanwhile pelts of armpit and leg hair are being proudly sported and embraced by the militantly liberated females.

As regards armpit hair, I'll offer a brief excerpt from an autobiographical book I am writing. This describes part of my first morning in Venezia, Italia, 1970:

"I remember climbing aboard one of those vaporettos and seeing a strange site, well, strange in one certain way. There was a young Italian man and his lady on one of the boats. (Nothing bizarre there; I was in Italy, after all.) She had short black hair and a dark gold face, her skin swarthy and radiant on a tight voluptuous body. Desirable to the extreme - especially to a two-nights sleepless, jet-lagged young guy like me who was out on his feet *yet* maniacally horny, which was totally in accordance with my habitually promiscuous soul. But what struck me, as soon as she raised her arms, was that she had a sharp, compact crop of jet-black *hair* under each one. Wow! Amazing! Horrible (Gasp!)! But… strangely… W.o.n.d.e.r.f.u.l…"

In America back in those days, a woman with hair under her arms would have been chased from the village or at the very least made the subject of Biker and Pollock jokes (actually I don't think Pollock jokes existed yet, but maybe they did). In Italy it was seemingly okay. Stunning, the effect it can have on you when you have been dealing with some kind of taboo all your life, and suddenly everyone says, "Hey, let's do it! Why not?" It's all the more amazing, because many of us then take a deep breath and jump in with both feet, as if into a strange lagoon of dark syrup. And come up for air feeling much better for taking the plunge.

Anyway, I found this woman intriguing. I mean, it's not like she had a nest full of bugs under her arms. But the darkness of the hair added to her Mediterranean glow - she was like a serpent wrapped around a mango - and gave her body an aura of almost intimidating freedom. Like, yes indeed…*a strange lagoon of dark syrup*. It made her the picture of sex, wild and fierce, this woman, long lost now, who belonged to another guy in another era, as so many of them do - the handsome man at her side who, I suspect, hadn't become bored with her yet, O, that morning which time has consumed!

She would be my age now, or older, maybe dead, and the passing thought is too bleak to dwell on. As I think about her now, her face is a blur, but I remember vividly those crisp shocks of sable adorning her Venetian armpits one long ago morning among the canals and cats and rats of the 'pearl of the Adriatic.'

On the other hand, I recall living in an apartment complex during my graduate school days in Gainesville, Florida. We were all neighbors and friends in this boxlike set-up which had a scruffy little yard in the middle that was just wide and long enough for a makeshift volleyball court. We all used to swill beer, devour doped-up brownies and play volleyball on the weekends. The Feminist Movement was alive and well even back then (1981-82), and one of the Feminist fads of the era was for young women to go bra-less (fifty claps from me for that) and to NOT shave their legs (which prompted the NOOOOOOOOO! buzzer from me).

There was an otherwise very attractive young lady, not terribly unlike that Italian woman in terms of her swarthy complexion, who would join us and who had let the hair grow up and down her legs. She was friendly, even vivacious, and rather sensuous, I suppose. Volleyball is a great sport for guys who enjoy watching braless women who are adequately endowed in the mammary department, and I daresay that even the most WOKE male unit of them all would have had difficulty in averting his eyes completely whenever Gina (as I will call her) sprang up to spike the ball over the net.

But the hairy legs... and boy they WERE hairy... were about as appetizing as a dude with a big five o'clock shadow shaving and then sprinkling the black nubs from his chin over a bowl of porridge. Or dust from a vacuum cleaner bag being emptied over a glass of milk and left floating on the top.

Gina was still salvageable because she was a great person. Even now I can offer no explanation aside from personal preference for how awful I thought it looked (though I am sure that the Sociologists and Psychologists could work it out). Probably something to do with my childhood. It just didn't fly for me. The hairy legs.

Finally, there is the issue of pubes. Soooooo much has changed since the days when I was a lounge lizard of lovers' lanes. Back then, none of the girls shaved, and some possessed a pubic mass bountiful enough to stuff LeBron James' Christmas stocking. THAT I found sexy, and when women started trimming it down, I was really put off at first. It seemed almost like having sex with a child, and that is one place (for all my character flaws and 'immoral' leanings) I would never go. It was like pulling off a woman's 'drawers' and discovering a skinhead lurking in them. With a slit from a razor blade on top.

But I got used to it. And you know, just as some men have more attractive dicks than others (I'm not gay either, at least not yet, but I have had 10,000 showers in locker rooms everywhere in Christendom following sports and fitness training , so I've seen all the junk in the warehouse. Some - even as a straight guy I can spot it clearly - are definitely the pick of the litter.), so are some women extremely beautiful 'down there.' Incredibly kissable-lickable just for starters in a way that all the public hair of yore somewhat detracted from. Also, back then, women often smelled bad. Just ignorance of proper hygiene I guess, because 9 out of 10 of the girls I knew placed a high value on cleanliness and all owned at least one bar of soap - but any older man will verify what I am saying. (It's where unseemly phrases like "stink finger" came from.)

Hope all this doesn't sound crude or insensitive. Not my intention. Just saying how it was…

The moral of the story? Anything can become fashionable if the fashion people keep after it long enough.

There was a time when guys who were going bald would do anything to hide the fact. Either slap on some dead-animal looking toupee' and clamp it down with pancake syrup until super glue was invented, or with a pair of tweezers tighten up on a few isolated strands and stretch them out strategically across the cranial runway like three different strains of a virus as seen under a microscope. All this as around the sides and backs of their heads a lingering mutton-chop crescent would hang, hedge-like, as if to preserve the "Look! I've still got some!" angle which these poor midlife crisis guys desperately hoped would somehow cause their secretaries to go moist.

I don't think any of it worked. Now guys, even teenagers with more hair atop their heads than brains inside them, when not waxing their chest and legs just peel it off and have done with it. Even the pubes. Makes their dicks look bigger and longer, they say. Whatever.

Even without dandruff, we are all helpless in the face of War, Politics, and Fashion. The only real problem I can see is that, bald or bushy, people seem about the same as ever. Bloodless social and corporate climbers on the one hand, ravenous, insatiable muff divers on the other.

MY NEW YORK CITY BLUES

One of the few really nice things about wandering around through life observing everything, even *wanting* everything, and yet never being able to hang on to any of it, is that nostalgia in its most seductively nebulous form infuses the spirit like an anonymous stranger. It's not individual *people* who always come to mind so much as what they were emblems of: crowds of *ghosts* - specters that inhabited your imagination to the point that you aren't really sure if they ever existed or not.

I think it's because we are never in control of the past. Rather, it controls *us* as gradually we disappear into the fading afternoons of life. Then we tell the stories we want told in the way we want them remembered. And hope nobody checks the record
too carefully.

So sometimes the past bites and sometimes it just sort of nibbles. Of course if you are a convicted murder in your 20th year of life-without- parole or have stood and watched while a car with your whole family in it went tumbling over a bridge to the rocks below, surely such things would stick in your mind in paralyzing detail. And no one knows better than I the *extremely* intense desire to go back and change certain moment-of-madness words and deeds. Occasions of wrath or ludicrous excess when an easily avoidable mistake ended a love affair or a friendship. A few of these failures still lodge in the recesses of my being like cancer in remission. From time to time something cruel hits me, and I still gasp.

Thus, like many another, I have made my way through life. Hellos and goodbyes, the usual assortment, only concerning different people, different faces than the ones you have known. Springtime buds and autumn leaves. Sometimes, like a great wind, a sigh surges through me when I contemplate these massive comings and goings. The brightening smiles like the door of heaven opening. The shocking nothingness at the end of the tunnel.

But, like the title of that Stephen King book, *Sometimes They Come Back.* And you never know when the moment of return will strike. You ask yourself: did the phone just ring or was it my imagination?

So, a pea-soup fog in a vanished Victorian street. A garishly bright enamel canvass, like an Edward Hopper painting where you can see the cracks in the soul rise to the surface of the skin.

A hotel lobby.

Someone…someone strides up to you out of a vision and, half-embarrassed, says: "Hello, it's ME again. Remember?" Bows and goes.

Yes, I mutter to the empty room. I remember.

I would like to go back to Manhattan, 1967. For some stupid, twisted reason, the first thing that comes to mind is that O.J. Simpson was playing for Southern Cal back then and I remember watching the Trojans go against UCLA in late November in a bar along Broadway with my friend Mike Boyle. As you know, O.J. later beat a murder rap when most people thought he was guilty. It caused a lot of hard feelings. But no one can say he wasn't one hell of a tailback. I remember that Saturday afternoon especially because at some point during the game, a Puerto Rican (I am thinking) woman walked into the bar from out of the Manhattan autumn and asked the guys sitting around if any of them wanted to have sex (payment please) with either of her daughters, aged 14 and 15. The game was hot, so no one took her up on it. Just kept on drinking their Shaeffers or Ballentine or Lowenbrau (the three brands of Manhattan back then). No one cared about being called a pedophile. Probably, if anyone had said the word, guys would have looked at them and said, "Huh?" The Age of Innocence.

I used to live in a place called the Hotel Lucerne on W. Broadway and 79th Street in New York City. That was in 1967.

They have cleaned up The Big Apple since then, or so they tell me. Legions of police keep order and corporate robots occupy organic food cafes. Times Square, which used to be infested with woebegone, drug-hooked, or just plain bad people, is now a Tourist Mecca. Everybody is eating sushi and doing yoga. Well, times change. But rumor has it that NYC has "lost its character." That's hard to define, but I get the meaning.

In reality, the old 'character' of Times Square was, among other treats, its giant porn houses. One time, stuck in Manhattan while waiting to go to the airport, I decided to pass a rainy afternoon watching the fuck films. When I entered the 'cinema' of my choosing, I expected a small shadowy room full of sickos and some sort of flickering camera shooting a dismal shaft of light onto a screen and sounding like a muffled heart-monitor in a woebegone hospital spitting out the fading rate of some loser's doomed ticker.

What I found instead was a palace. High ceilings and chandeliers like a Circle Line Moscow Metro station. They could have performed a ballet there in that masturbatory Super Dome. Because, sure enough, it was porn all the way. But...what a throng! When I think back, I sort of imagine that this is how cyberspace must be, you know, when all of those people, thousands of them evidently, play computer competitions all night. A different world. Do these worlds really exist, and was this real - Manhattan, Times Square, middle of the afternoon? Yes, because.

The human mind has many galleries. Most of them gather dust as you age. But sometimes, as on a twilight street, you go back and polish the faded pictures.

So I started thinking about those old New York days recently, and right away the Hotel Lucerne popped into my brain.

I had come to New York with a high school friend of mine from Minnesota. No reason really, except that these were the '60s - the Days of Dylan, so to speak - and Greenwich Village was a 'happening' place. I wanted to be part of the scene. Why we chose the Hotel Lucerne as our headquarters I have long since forgotten, but I guess everyone always ends up somewhere. Probably because it was cheap by New York standards, or maybe Mike and I simply happened to be wandering around in that direction and tripped over a drunk crashed out on the street near the entrance. It sure as hell wasn't on any travel brochure because, frankly, it was a bit of a dump.

Not that it was empty. Anything but. It was as crowded as the subway, day and night. I suppose the Hotel Lucerne could best be described as a 'transient' hotel, by which I mean an establishment where people (sometimes whole families) came and went very often. At 3 a.m., the elevator was likely to be packed. It was one of those places - its lobby was big and drafty yet vaguely smelling of human sweat, and anchored with a jaded carpet that seemed centuries old - where even in the middle of the afternoon it always seemed like the middle of the night. Full of immigrant-looking people with stony faces who invariably appeared tired but somehow in a hurry. Like they had just come off the boat. As I hailed from West Virginia, which was full of hillbillies (toothless Appalachian goofballs whose toddlers ran around with shit hanging out of their diapers), so all these hawklike Slavs and Spaniards seemed pretty exotic to me, especially the slouching mahogany-colored women. You would not exactly have said they were beautiful - not if by 'beautiful' you mean the girls on the cover of Cosmopolitan magazine – but to me they seemed distantly seductive and, in some cases, hardcore erotic. Without trying in the least to be. Like cold dark cabinets of flesh, but with burning ovens under their dresses. Or so I dreamed in my Hee-Haw West Virginia way.

Anyhow, Mike and I moved in, and then we both got jobs at the New York Public Library. That's where our paths began to diverge. Mike was assigned to the branch at Lincoln Center -

where there was a lot of culture, such as art and ballet - and I was sent to the division on Lenox Avenue and 132nd Street. It was in the middle of Harlem, which In those days was the biggest ghetto for black people in NYC. I wanted it. This was the Civil Rights era, and I had a bad case of Jungle Fever. I entertained a naive but very romantic view of the black lifestyle and I had the hots for black women. To me, going to Harlem to work made a lot of sense.

Always the activist in romantic pursuits, I soon found myself frequenting a juke dive called the Bluepoint Cafe up on 96th Street. It was full of Negroes (which you could say back then), and, as a matter of fact, I was usually the only spot of milk in the joint. Not surprising therefore that one fine evening, I was approached at the bar by a winsome colored lady (it was also still okay to say 'colored') wearing a 'processed' (smooth-haired) wig who introduced herself as 'Rita' and sweetly informed me that, for a small fee, she could enrich my night by leaps and bounds. It was an offer I couldn't refuse. We went somewhere, and I still remember, telling her - upon finding out the that the "small fee" was not so small after all - that "I think they would charge less in West Virginia," and her saying (sweetly), "Honey, this ain't West Virginia."

Everything went well. In fact, it went so goddamned well that one night in the witching hours (about 4 a.m.) she turned up at the Hotel Lucerne looking for me. (I had told her where I stayed and what room. Didn't think it mattered.) I guess I must have been flattered because I gave her the royal welcome. Mike wasn't so happy. He got over it that time, maybe even grudgingly considered it cool that an 18-year-old out-of-towner like me could pull an obvious hooker in off the street. I never told him I had paid for it, and, anyway, this time there was no small fee at all; she was just down on her luck and looking for a place to stay. After that she would come and go. At all hours. Mike was less and less amused, and finally he just got mad and moved the hell out. *Arrivederci,* Mike.

I soon discovered that Rita was basically a lesbian and that she had a drug habit. Even then, at that tender age, I somehow wasn't the least bit shocked. Heaven knows where I got this strange side of my character from, but - although in this life I have been invited to some pretty ritzy places now and then - always there has lurked in me a peculiar love of the slums, a submission to the allure of darkening people and bleak places. Rita was a 'nighthawk,' no more, no less. I unblinkingly accepted it. I loved the sugar that was rotting in her breath... As I said, she came and went. No telling when or where.

Meanwhile at the Countee Cullen Library, I often spent time down in the basement pasting jackets to hold the 'borrowing' cards in the backs of books. Remember, it was a long time ago. All this digital stuff was a long way off. One day I saw a volume called *Lady Sings the Blues*, and it was a ghost-written autobiography of Billie Holiday, the great blues singer from an earlier era. The story of her life, unfolding as it did in her own (fictitious) voice and catty, jivey way of talking, completely mesmerized me. Then, having digested the sad, rocky tale (she was dead by then - of drugs and alcohol), I decided that I needed to hear what she sounded like. So I combed the record shops along Broadway until I found a Billie Holiday album. I bought it and took it home. But I had no record player. I bought one. Cheap as I could find.

But let me tell you something about the room at the hotel. It was strictly old world, like something from the 1920s. There was no view from the window except for the facade of the building opposite, below (I was up on a high floor) was an alley. Sometimes people in the rooms above me would throw stuff out the window and I could watch it come sailing down. Every now and then someone would even piss out the window and I could watch that too, tumbling in a nice sharp stream. There was a metal hot plate for cooking, and that was all. No fridge... no TV.
Rita used to bring women with her once in a while, usually in a fucked-up state. I remember one big fat one who was so far gone she could hardly move. How Rita ever even got her into the

elevator, I'll never know. As I told you, she was a junkie. I didn't understand much about it. She would take out these wrappers full of powder, mix it with water, then take a syringe and shoot it in the web between her thumb and index finger. Always the same place. I didn't mind, and that's the strange thing about me, I guess. She might as well have pulled out a box of animal crackers.

One night she gave me one of those packets to snort. No needle, just a snort. And it was a miracle. I never felt so good. I spent the rest of the night alternatively licking her out (which is what she loved) and just talking with her - about our lives, our childhoods...we found a few hours of real intimacy...until the morning of Manhattan crept between the shades, and she got up and went out to catch the morning trade.

Gradually I started to get tired of Rita. One night she left, promising to come back, and never returned. *Arrivederci,* Rita.

Thanksgiving was near and I was damn near broke. So I asked one of the colored girls who worked the corner in front of the Chock-Full-o-Nuts coffee shop on the edge of Broadway what I could buy cheap that would fill me up. She evidently came from the South because she immediately suggested 'grits' - a cornmeal type of Kaшa that they like with breakfast down in Alabama and Georgia, etc. So I went hunting for grits. Turns out anything you want is available in New Yawk City! Came Thanksgiving night and I went back to the Hotel Lucerne to celebrate with my grits and a big jug of wine. The festivities were going to be marked by the first grand performance of Billie Holiday because I had just bought the record player with the last of my paycheck.

It was freezing cold out on those windy late November streets, and I was shivering when I got back. But then - as now sometimes - the alcohol solved the problem. I was feeling good and a little nostalgic (it comes with the wind and the rain). I figured I would munch down some of those grits and listen to the music. Trouble was I had never cooked grits before and so I didn't have any idea how much to dump into the saucepan. Turned out I put in half the bag and that was almost half a bag too much. The water was boiling as I slurped the wine and stirred my Thanksgiving dinner. And then, to my horror, the shit started foaming up and billowing out over the sides of the pot and spilling all over the goddamned floor. It was the god-awfullest mass of albino bowel-movement you ever saw. And it tasted like washing powder. The hell with dinner.

I took another gulp of 'juice' and sat down to put on the music. I guess I was half-crocked by then, and sure enough, just as I looked up, here came the jet of piss streaking past my window-pane. Right on time. Rather sad. Then, from her grave, came the voice of Billie Holiday, and I have never forgotten that moment. To tell the truth, 'Lady Day,' as she was sometimes known, didn't turn out to be my favorite blues/jazz singer. Her voice is too…watery…somehow. I've heard Nina Simone and Etta James songs that I like better. But on this particular evening - bone-cold outside on the streets and barren inside my soul - that voice gave the ultimate comfort. "God Bless the Child that Got His Own" is the name of that song. You should listen to it sometime.

As I have grown older, I seem to have forgotten how to cry. Alcohol helps, of course. And probably I cried some that evening, too. Don't know if it was me crying or the wine. I sure was missing Rita about then. But, like I said, it was cold outside, and, anyway, New York is too big to go looking for someone. And forever is a long time to be gone.

ALL-NIGHT DINERS AND ETERNAL DARKNESS

There is a famous painting by the American Edward Hopper called *Nighthawks* which I ran across on the internet a couple of days ago. I love the frigid melancholy of much of Hopper's work and suggest to my readers that you check him out if you have never heard of him before.

Nighthawks depicts a late-night diner cafe in New York City in 1942. Four people are in the diner: a man sitting with a woman, another man with his back to us, and a young guy working behind the counter. The men have on dark blue suits and are also wearing the fedora hats that 'business' men (of all description), private detectives, and criminals, etc., wore during that era. (Check out a Bogart film to get the idea.)

The woman is coldly attractive in the way of late, dead-end nights. Her long, swept hair is ginger-colored, and she has on a red evening dress. She appears to be examining the fingernails on her right hand - always a sign of female ambiguity. The man whose back we see sits isolated with shoulders hunched - maybe a gangster of some sort, but we don't know. The boyish guy behind the counter is wearing a white sailor suit sort of get-up (the company uniform), with a little beret type of lid perched on his head. He seems busy about his work, but, again, as fixed in time and place as a frozen mannequin caught in mid-motion.

The cafe' is bright, like Van Gogh's *Night Cafe* or the idea we may have from Hemingway's short story "A Clean, Well-lighted Place." In Hopper's painting there is no door visible; it is rather as though the inhabitants of the diner are locked inside, maybe for eternity.

The smooth street outside, surrounded by softly firestone, implacably statuesque buildings, is silent, uninhabited. The city, representing the world outside the diner, is all the more stark, forbidding, and ghostly because of its implicit desolation juxtaposed against the hard enamel precision of the people in the painting, who are both fully conceived and absolutely empty, and the reflecting emptiness of the street, simultaneously terminal and eternal, means that, wherever they have come from to get to here, there is really nowhere else for them to go.

In this night-cafe, the world ends, the world stops not with a bang or a whimper, but with menacing ennui. This night will never cease, the invisible, inaudible gramophone's needle is stuck in time.

I have been in cafes and diners like that before, often also in the dead of night - sometimes sober, often drunk, sometimes with a place to go to afterwards, and once or twice with nowhere definite in mind. Do you know of them - the nights when, wherever you happen to find yourself, the place is full of lonely souls and people with dark ambitions, women of many nightmares, insomniacs of all description, freaks of every assortment. These decadent die-hards, these violin-players with shaky hands, these ghostly mimics of the Moulin Rouge, they have their only chance at 3 o'clock in the morning. I know because I have been there too, I have been one of them.

In these night cafes, there seems to be sanctuary, even communion, among the greyhound bus rabble, the destitute pilgrims who never found anywhere, never located their own holy grail. In these places people tend to behave themselves, a least for a while, before heading off into whatever oblivion they choose... until the discoloring and racking realities of morning's sallow light gobble them up. They have come to pause and suck up a little breath before facing the night-wind.

Back in 1967, when I lived in New York City on W. 79th Street, I used to sit in the "Chock-Full-o-Nuts" coffee shop most of the night and work on the stories I was writing and sometimes talk to the black prostitutes who stood on the street outside waving at potential tricks gliding by in their cars. They were young and wore high boots and straight-haired (or 'processed') wigs. A lot of them had heroin habits, and with their johns I guess they would do most anything.

But on rainy winter evenings, or on those late lazy summer nights of dying sunlight in Manhattan, they would slink or bound (depending on their mood) into the diner and sit for a spell, drinking coffee and smoking cigarettes, which was allowed back then. Some of them would notice the strange little white boy hunched there night after night, and venture to say hello.

Well, that's all they had to do. Saying hello to me has **always** been like opening the floodgates, and so I got to know some of those women pretty well. Maybe I was like a mascot. But what I found was this: they were all just plain people in the end, people who really wanted to come in out of the rain, people who didn't really like having turned into the nowheresville ghouls they had become. And so when they talked to me, they just knew I wasn't some pimp or drug dealer, Not even a potential trick. I was only a kid from West Virginia, just like they were from Tennessee or North Carolina. And so we talked like normal people and we were the briefest of friends.

It was because the cafe was a sanctuary, a safe house. Maybe it was somehow like the title of that John Le Carre novel, *The Spy Who Came in from the Cold.*

I thought then, and I think now, that whoever you are, you need a place to come in from the cold.

Like the truckers who drive long hours across Europe, Russia, Canada, and the United States. And, I suppose, everywhere in the **world** even China and India. It must be lonely, out there in those great rigs, driving from Denver to Pittsburgh, from Glasgow to London, from Ontario to Alberta. It must get damned lonely.

But as **long** as there are truck stops along the way, you can make it, right? Bacon and eggs, coffee and camaraderie, a pretty waitress with a saucy smile and exposed cleavage - the tastes and smells of humanity in a single room where the food is hot, the coffee hotter. This is protection from the wolfish darkness out in the parking lot and beyond. Of course, there are girls waiting in the shadows to accommodate the truckers. For a price. There are always night-hawks waiting in the crevice-like wrinkles of the eternal seam, and they are always available for a price. The bacon and eggs come cheaper. And better.

Likewise, when I was a raw, green, punk child of West Virginia, my grandfather (who took me in after my parents' divorce), would sometimes pack me and my granny in the car and take us from Martinsburg to Morgantown, which back then meant 9 hours of driving over windy, mountainous roads of two-lane blacktop. We would stop in nondescript towns along the way for toilet and gas. But for some reason we always paused for lunch in a place called Sutton. The same restaurant, the same proprietor. He was a basic country man with a toothpick constantly wedged between his teeth. He knew my grandfather from previous trips, and so he was always friendly. As friendly as the owner of a small diner in the middle of nowhere could be expected to be. He is still there, of course, but now in
a time-bubble.

My portion of food, as I vaguely recall, consisted of a hamburger and French fries and Coca-Cola. Afterwards, the long journey would start again. Sometimes I would get what they called "car sick" and they would have to pull over for me to vomit. When you are a child, nine hours in a car can seem as long as it takes for school to be out in the spring when it's only February. I would wish I was back in Sutton, still nibbling on my burger.

My mother, in the days when she was young, knew some Greek people in Martinsburg, and this Greek family ran a restaurant called "Louise's". I ate a lot of greasy plates of food in that establishment. But, again, I felt safe and secure inside, because I could watch and hear my beautiful, perfect mom chatting with her friends. It was 1955 and the Brooklyn Dodgers were about to beat the mighty New York Yankees in the World Series. There wasn't anything wrong with the world back then that I knew of. I can still see Charlie, the cook with one glass eye, spitting on the grill to check if it was hot, and hear my mother complain with disgust, "We must eat his spit."

Big Chevrolets and Pontiacs and Mercuries and Packards were parked outside in the sun-sprinkled streets of that long-lost era. And serious-looking men in fedora hats passed along the street. The women back then were not emaciated like the rail-thin catwalk types today. Personally, I have never had a fixation on big breasts, but back then there seemed to be a lot more tit and cleavage. Women like Marilyn Monroe and Jayne Mansfield set the tone. The women then, as I recall them, were just fleshier - if that makes any sense. They would sit along counters and smoke cigarette after cigarette, their pumps dangling from the foot of whichever leg they had crossed, revealing the rich trails of shadow between their toes.

But even then, we were all nighthawks. Those little restaurants and cafes, well, they saved us from a bigger world, a grander universe. They spared us the impossible things we didn't want to think about and couldn't have fathomed anyway.

Amid smells of bacon and burger and coffee and ginger ale, we bought ourselves a few hours of insulation from what was out there and beyond.

Death seemed far, far away. But I understand now that, even in the bright daytime back then in Martinsburg, where the young women wore splotches of crimson lipstick like remnants of cherry pie over their ordinary but vaguely pretty faces, those ambitious small-town women of limited ingenuity who always seemed to end up marrying alcoholic guys named Fred and Sam - I know now that it was always night-time. I know because they still come to me in dreams, but only in the dead of night when something buried in me needs these confused memories to be awakened. Then one of those women comes and rubs her bare foot slowly over my face.

Like something out of Aladdin's lamp, all of those people snap back to life suddenly in a way that in some dreamers would promote fear, but even knowing that they are ghosts, I am not afraid of them. I want them. I couldn't see it clearly then, but now I do. What looked like daytime was really the middle of the night. It was 4 a.m. when my grand-folks or my mother and I went to those cafes and sat along the counter-tops, cafes where there were no doors at all - only the grease, fries and cola, and maybe a peppy little guy wearing the company cap, supposedly making sodas but always frozen to his spot under ceiling lights that seemed bright in the everlasting darkness.

THE GRACEFUL VERTIGO OF THE SKY NOODLES

Long ago I stood atop the Empire State Building and peered down at Manhattan, where, to understate the matter slightly, there seemed to be a lot going on. Miniscule bags of brain, bugs with motors, horns shouting up at the haze like mad hunters firing at the sky. For a moment I felt like an Olympian giant staring down at a frenzy of squiggles, feeling a mixture of wonder and contempt. Probably to them, if they had looked up - but why would they? - they would have seen, not my own myopic smear of a face, but, attached to the edge of the ledge, a tiny chunk of something-or-other: a discarded wad of gum? A hardened boil of baked snot? A rat who had wandered in and out of an elevator and was now confused? It's only my experience talking here, my guess at how most tourists to the top of the Empire State Buildings and the citizens below imagine each other. One hamster gazing at a million other hamsters.

To be honest, I was not alone. There were other people in my midst, as many as could be safely crammed onto the more than adequately barricaded and fortified top of what was then the tallest beanstalk in the world. It was to keep people from jumping off, because - as you know - people do the darned-est things, don't they?

Both the Empire State Building and the Golden Gate Bridge have coaxed more than a few to take the plunge. We all, sooner or later - Hamlets all in our own right - become aware of suicide as an option. The startling thing is how many young people grab it and go with it. HEY, Parents and Facebook friends, Look at ME: Dead!!! Most of us gaze in horrified amazement at this strangely tempting old Wallenda inside ourselves wobbling upon his last tightrope before disappearing from sight. Not exactly suicide, but rather what some call 'a death wish.' But a few people, from the start, embrace the cackle in the void. For them, it's just a matter of time.

There is a famous photograph which captured what was dubbed as "The Most Beautiful Suicide," taken by Robert Wiles and capitalized on by Andy Warhol. It looks staged, but I can assure you that it is oh, so real.

That was back in 1947. I even did some research into the life of the dead woman. Her name was Evelyn McHale and she was a bookkeeper. Like certain personality types which ultimately make little sense to the rest of us, she was one of those in whom the last peaceful valley of stone seemed to beckon from the beginning. I guess she also had a taste for melodrama.

But as I stood way up there on that distant day, I was not thinking about anybody named Evelyn McHale. I was having one of those moments. You know the kind. It is the moment of ultimate understanding, when all the depths rush up to greet you, and when you grasp your own essence in some tangible, 'objective' correlative. Like when I went to Europe as a dreamy youth long ago when the Atlantic Ocean was the great grey way leading to the cobbled streets and twisting alleys of my European imaginings; when the Atlantic was not yet a mere 'global' river with all waves leading to one McDonald's or another in some tourist and immigrant packed Eurotrash city-du-jour.

And when, back in 1970, I walked out of the train station in Venezia, still jet-lagged and bleary-eyed from a sleepless night in a noisy *cuccetta* in the train down from Luxembourg City...and, by dawn made only of ghost material, floated straight into the Renaissance.

Or crossed the English Channel years later on the jetfoil under a purple morning sky and decided it was the conveyance of a medieval army taking me back to Cornwall or Devon. Moments when ghosts of all kinds nibble like wild birds on the scarecrow in your soul.

And then the Empire State Building. I must have been 14.

Looming 1,250 feet over the middle of Manhattan, It had been the world's tallest building from 1931 until the first World Trade Tower was completed in 1970. Thus, being one of a kind, if you stood on top, there was nothing on the face of the earth to look up at. Only the sun, the moon, the stars at night.

It started in the 1920s when New York was roaring, and the stock market's lid hadn't blown off yet. Actually, it was a competition of sorts. Wall Street's Bank of Manhattan Building and the Chrysler Building, "a monument to me," according to Walter Chrysler, the car mogul. What a guy. Then former Mayor Al Smith and General Motors executive John J Raskob got into the act, and the Empire State Building became a reality. In fact, it was built at the speed of light: four and a half stories per week, using 3,400 men each day for 20 months.

After the stock market crashed, followed by the Great Depression, the building was only 25% occupied. They started calling it 'The Empty State Building." Workers would leave the lights on in the upper floors to create the illusion that it was a bustling business center. (This reminds me of when cell phones first came out. Purchasers would pay extra to receive 'phantom' calls to make it look like they were important people much in demand.) It wasn't until after WW11 that the huge building started to pay for itself.

Over the years, many unlikely stories have helped define the existence of the great building. For one thing - as much as we rue 9/11, it was not the first time an aircraft plowed into the side of a skyscraper. On 28 July, 1945 a U.S. military plane - a bomber no less - got lost in the fog on its way to LaGuardia airport and rammed into the 78th and 79th floors, killing the pilots and 11 people in the building. As result of the explosion, an elevator went plunging 75 floors with a woman onboard who miraculously survived, probably due to the air pressure from below slowing the speed of the descending cubicle. She broke her back and neck but did not die.

Another: for a while back in the day, it was thought that zeppelins could dock near the top of the building, sort of like a space station or satellite system, I suppose; this was when transatlantic airships were considered the wave of the future. Further, it was believed that passengers could enter the Empire State Building via a special gangway and descend right into mid-Manhattan via special elevators - not the free falling but fast as 'greased lightning,' as they used to say - within 7 minutes);.

Then there was the King Kong doll (larger than life when inflated and attached to the building) which was meant as a publicity stunt to promote the famous film, but unfortunately kept ripping open, and after a couple repair attempts, they just shit-canned the idea.

Also, several daredevils have parachuted from various high floors. The cops were waiting below to haul them off to the clink, though a couple managed to escape - and good for them. Well, that's the human race for you in a nutshell, don't you think? Fabulous both in conception and in folly.

But that's where my interest in the Empire State Building ends. It was one of the Ruthian Yankee Stadiums of its time, and that time is gone.

What continues is the human obsession with climbing higher and higher. And higher.

If you look at photos - or happen to go there yourself - of the great modern megalopolises - monster-cities of over 20,000,000 inhabitants, you will also notice, standing side-by-side-by-side, stem-by-stem, a sky-rocketing host of steel candles, fire glinting in some of the upper windows as they approach the sun. This is also true in not-so-populated but specially manufactured 'attractions' such as Dubai and other contemporary meccas of the Arab world where the emphasis now is apparently not on fossil fuels but on real estate.

Accordingly, we can easily dispense with the practical reasons for building high and tall. Early on, it was the inventions of the telephone, the typewriters, and the creation of the universal US postal service which brought about the need for more office space, for people now rushed into the urban centers by subway trains, trams, and elevated rail links. Improvements in steel fortifications, sprinkling systems to supply higher floors with water, and advanced electronics, were also essential in the birth of the modern skyscraper.

Beyond that, my questions take a different turn, heading in the direction of alternative human needs beyond that which engineering ingenuity and advanced technology can bring to bear. You know, they just get higher and higher and more and more plentiful, and in some of them there are not offices as much as just people living there. Imagine that: imagine *living* in a building a half mile above the ground, looking down on the clouds as if they were snowdrifts.

Looking down that day from the Empire State Building I remember being amazed by the blind simultaneity of events - although, of course, at 14 I wouldn't have expressed it that way. But the reason was clear to me, then as now. I saw how what might have been occurring on one street had nothing to do with what could have been going on the next street over: in one a wedding celebration, in the other a heart attack. Everywhere oblivion and indifference; by contrast an anthill is a friendly neighborhood. But I also wondered who was actually heading for whom, whether by design, fate, or chance, and how such meetings would play out. For some few, today would be like no other day, while for others it would be nothing more than a tasteless substance smeared on a napkin, or maybe the smudge from a woman's lipstick, or maybe a name or phone number soon discarded and forgotten. All this I saw from the top of the Empire State Building.

Now of course, the Empire State Building is diminished, dwarfed as it is by the many other superior skyscrapers of the world: the sky-walking human ego cloning itself again and again, a symbolically aroused squadron of lanky porn stars made of steel and glass measuring each other's penile amplitude in a studio of sky; or stoic, graceful, deadly serpents poised to give poisonous bites to the moon and sun; or electricity-charged noodles bobbing and listing on windy days, all erect and standing at attention in massive bunches in the form of architectural cylinders like clusters of rocket ships on their launching pads, eager to assault the stars.

Human longing has led to the crossing of many frontiers, and maybe the only ones left are *out there* somewhere, and the skyscrapers, their high tips often disappearing in the morning mists and the evening haze of the megapolis, seem to know this, as if they suddenly had minds of their own.

As I remember how I surmised those little human dots and toy cars racing about on their ant-like errands below the Empire State Building, I am reminded by a line uttered by a character named Harry Lime in a book called *The Third Man*. He is riding in a Ferris wheel overlooking Vienna, and he asks the woman sitting next to him, "Would you really feel pity if one of those dots stopped moving forever?"

My answer would be No, not really. If they all stopped....I suppose I would wonder what to do next, there as I wandered the vibrating hallways of my windy tower. Maybe the stopping of the dots would frighten me, and I would wonder what plague or chemical gas has brought them to such stillness. And then I would check my refrigerator.

Maybe that - or something like it - compels people to live in such towers. Of course many skyscrapers house only business offices, but a lot of others are for private residences - somehow more imposingly secluded than the offices of any rich man's exclusive country club - and so upwards, upwards go the elite denizens of such a mentality, upwards into their strange skyboxes that transcend the growling congestion of the miasma below because, as the skyscrapers rise to their ever-higher peaks, at some point they simply disconnect from the rest of what is going on.

And they will grow higher and higher, so I am told. I have read interesting articles about how indeed they sway about somewhat at their tops when the wind is strong (I felt this effect in a high building in Prague once) - but they are constructed admirably so as not to fall over. Likewise, I am informed that there can be problems with the elevators/lifts that shoot them up *bistro-bistro* like a slide in a waterpark turned upside down or toothpaste being squeezed violently from a tube. I can imagine the blood rushing from my head and vertigo blotting me out. Deep-sea divers can get 'the bends' if they come too quickly to the surface from great depths. Could we get the bends from rocketing up too quickly on one of these elevators?

And what are the real motives behind wishing to live way up there in such a place? I think it is because...*in truth*...we have all just given up on each other. I have detected among humans a shrinking from rhetoric and discourse to mere slogans and sound-bites. We have become - at least those who can afford to - more reductive, more minimalist. Imagine, if you can, a person who - once gregarious, even vivacious - gradually separates from other people and seeks refuge among his dogs or cats or parrots. Or maybe his hamsters. And then those also are carried away and replaced by replicas lacquered up in their inner dials with Artificial Intelligence. Ultimately, he withdraws even from his friendliest robots as they wag their tails, and seeks out the company of his plants, only to discover that they too are now technological chips with *minds* of their own. In the end we find him stooped over his desk with a microscope, contemplating the complexities of a follicle of his own hair to see if it is real hair or the hair of someone trapped inside a video game created by a being far far away. There must be a reason; he wishes to believe and to know this reason.

Isn't this sort of *disaffiliation* the object of many of the strange pilgrims in the modern world, an 'atlas shrugged' mentality in a very literal sense? Shrugging off the world. And maybe without so much as a sigh.

And would it be too much of a stretch to suggest that the obsession we have in the present day with social media, smart phones, etc., is based on the same impulse: a means of living in the world, *within* but from *outside* it at the same time? Seizing on all the 'things' of the world, including its people, without ever having to really touch them and in so doing soil our hands with their germs and become nauseated by ingesting the sour breath they exhale in the form of unbearable human exhaust emission??

Imagine a man or woman, as garishly lonely as someone in an Edward Hopper painting, hunched over a computer way up on Floor No. 256, poring over thousands of pages of data, rather like the hermit in the woods who spends his life studying the train schedules to and from all the big cities?

Skyscrapers in their own splendid, deity-like, yet starkly introverted way, accomplish infinitely more than social media in terms of defining the meaning of *isolation.* They are as one observer, a writer called Jane Jacobs, noted, like "streets piled high in the sky." Others have referred to their inhabitants' "boxed-in lives" - when they are used for residential purposes. It seems the way of the world: those who *can* isolate, so often *do.* But why? Or is that a silly question?

Since all of us obviously have to be somewhere at all times, which is the more powerful experience: standing at the bottom, on the street among 'Gooners' gazing up, or standing at the top, looking down?

I recall a short but very powerful poem I heard long years ago from one member of what were known as 'The Liverpool Poets'. It went like this:

> 'One thing I have learned about life:
> you cannot possess the citadel from the outside.'

Only that. But again the question is based on perspective, and if - as my brief relationship with the Empire State Building revealed to me - these perspectives take the form of opposite mirrors, each evoking the other as a distant vision harboring what the imagination might crave as its desired reality , then... no matter at which end of the spectrum you find yourself, your restless dreaming wish will be to achieve the other.

In cities we live our lives in the midst of great noise, such as that which riots every minute in the thoroughfares, but.many of us, in our secret selves, long for silence - the kind you would surely find atop the Matterhorn, and indeed of a kind which is possible to feel atop a skyscraper - or EVEN MORE in one of those taller taller taller buildings which dwarf even the ancient skyscrapers - a high sanctuary beyond birds where you can escape onto one of the upper balconies and gaze down, until all noise from down below subsides, and nothing remains but the cacophonies disturbing your own daydreams. And amnesia- bringing gales.

Except that one day something unidentified comes tumbling down from above. What was it? Someone's casually disposed of refuse? Another suicide?

Listen. There is nothing. My soul is tired. Please, someone, MAKE A NOISE!!!

Skyscraper. The ultimate shout of human greatness; the ultimate, majestic symbol of human loneliness.

These peerless beanstalks were a novelty once, but no longer. In places like Dubai and Hong Kong they are manifest in growing multitudes.

I had a student some years back who went to Vietnam on holiday. On his way he stopped over in Hong Kong. He had taken a lot of photographs, and naturally I wanted to see them - not so much the ones of Vietnam (although I was curious about that, too, because of my memories of the "Vietnam period" in

American life) but most particularly those of the great Chinese City, for which I had long held some fanciful but treasured emotions, dreaming of it as a venerable, wisdom-permeated juggle of tilting houses and slopes of narrow streets retained from a magical Chinese past.

But it wasn't so. The photos revealed a skyline jumbled with manifold skyscrapers. It was almost as if they represented in art-form slippery and stark, some kind of tall-stemmed virus which had learned to duplicate itself over and over.

Skyscrapers for some reason suggest to me the presence of a delicious pornography circulating among blanched angels, a stratospheric cry of "SUCCESS!" - these hermit-like cathedrals of modern hubris. But in the early morning when the dawn in red delight creeps out of the sky or silver evening comes with its shadows, the skyscrapers can seem strangely ancient. Like predatory birds at rest.

And so, in the great cities, rather like in Alfred Hitchcock's film *The Birds,* we see them cluster, more and more and more, and hover there, sinewy reptiles of glass and steel among whose dreaming corridors, one may gather, the strangest things are happening - or maybe nothing is happening at all, or just some lonely cleaner or executive - Towers of Babel but without voices - snake-noodles rising, in frightening fecundity, out of their boxes, in answer to the strains of a magic flute.

THE DAWNS AND TWILIGHTS OF OFFICES

*"What did I know, what did I know
Of love's austere and lonely offices?"*
© ROBERT HAYDEN, THOSE WINTER SUNDAYS

Somehow, I found myself reading ancient Chinese poetry translated into English. This was years ago. The other day I tried to relocate some of those verses, but not a chance. There was plenty of ancient Chinese poetry to be had, but not the ones I remembered.

Here is why I wanted to find them. The poems were very short, no more than little glimpses into the life and emotions of some man who lived more than 2500 years ago - well before the time Christ is said to have come along. But the translator had come up with the ingenious idea of translating the little poems in such a way that they seem almost chatty without losing any of their pathos; the speaker in the poems is accessible, indeed contemporary. But there is a longing in his voice, a sadness...or is it only my own sadness superimposed? Plus my knowledge that this man and the woman he wished to go home to vanished long, long ago.

Some artists become ornaments to an era; others speak through time. In such voices, where they speak through words, paint, marble or music, the freshness of expression never fades. Think for a moment about the speaker in Corinthians 13:12: "For now we see through a glass, darkly; but then face to face: now I know in part; but then I shall know even as I am also known." Every time I see these lines, Paul the Apostle, lean, fierce, and worn by the world, is in the room with me. I am not religious in any definable sense, and I despise a lot of what Christianity has done (mostly by one 'Christian' to another).

But I hear Paul the man.

And so, regarding the Chinaman of that distant epoch, what got me was the way this frayed and harried guy, stuck at work and longing to be home with his wife, complained about having to spend so much time at the office. And "office" was the word he kept using (thanks to the translator's grasp of how to get it across). The Chinaman could have been any one of us - stuck in our own offices, but there he was, back in some ancient province of a culture as old as stone and dirt, sounding just like us. A man from the mist, but in a room we know.

You can look at it two ways. As a cynic, you can say, well it just goes to show you that nothing has changed and to look at the past romantically is like gazing with wistful eyes at chamber pots brimming with piss, cemeteries roaring with the sound of whirling flies and other buzz-bombing insects, and sex drowned in a nostril-searing inferno of putrid smells amid the pinching clutch of bedbugs. And it would be true if you imagine yourself in any medieval or even 'Renaissance' town.

You could say that. But some of us would still go. Back to those streets. Back to *those* offices. We would go in search of something elusive which the history books never tell us but which the painters and poets do. We - some of us, that is - would seek out that hard, smelly, raunchy old world... Why? To drink wine while the virgins danced around the Maypole? To be spectators at grisly public executions? In hopes of bumping into Chaucer or Leonardo in some faded street of a distant day long since eaten by Time? To verify something in ourselves, some connecting rod in us that needs validation?

Or is it the unshakeable belief that something about Cleopatra and Antony floating down the Nile was simply better than (take a quick look around you if you happen to be standing in a shopping mall, 2021)... than *all this shit*? That an illiterate milkmaid of five centuries ago in some rocky English village would have answered your dreams better than Megan the Social Justice Warrior shaking her fist at Your Racist Homo-trans-Islama-phobic Cisgender Ass?

Well, I guess you can look over Marlowe's "Come Live With Me" poem and Raleigh's sardonic reply - and decide which world is the world for you.

Ah, the office. At such times as when your Partner or Significant Other is riding you like a cowboy on a longhorn bull in a rodeo, the office is the great escape. "Honey," you say to the Ball and Chain, "I have to go to the office." Or sometimes you just stay late, even when the work is done. And you look out at the gleaming city, imagining yourself in the arms of a million different women, all without distinct faces but possessing a tremendous allure. It makes you nostalgic for the things never done, the people never met, the lovers never found. (Excuse me, but I'm a guy.)

O-f-f-i-c-e... What to make of this word that defines so much of our lives? It is not a pretty word. Like "zephyr." Or "rhododendron" or "nightingale." Or even "cunnilingus". I prefer the word 'ennui' (pronounced 'on-wee'). I saw a painting once with that title: "Ennui of the Afternoon" - and what did it show but a great grid of streets lying flat and compliant beneath the opaque blocks of big buildings, and in the midst of it all was a stupendous, human-shattering silence. The silence of human creation coupled with the silence of the universe: this was the ennui of the afternoon. But there were offices everywhere. They proliferated like one dying man's cries echoing amid a thousand others. But you could hear nothing and everywhere were shadows made of steel.

O-f-f-i-c-e. But in this brief locution that sounds a bit like the "oink" of a pig, much, so very much, of the modern world is contained. For multitudes of people, the interior of some office holds more chapters of their lives than any seashore or forest or mountain. Or home.

In these offices, the outcomes of whole careers are determined. Sometimes love affairs take place after hours on office couches. Cognac is pulled from the drawer if you are The Boss. In offices, pressure and deadlines dictate the rate at which beats the human heart and blood-flow as it spills through human veins. In such offices, especially in today's corporate culture, more masks are worn than at a Halloween Ball. So, in this sense, the office is a place of eternal falsehood and deception, no less than the streets outside. A place where human engines tune their motors and refine their skill at pretending to be someone other than who they really are.

And yet, it could be argued, it *is* who they really are.

There is, or used to be, the retirement ceremony of offices, for the sake of those who had grown old in their office. Think back, old man: the young highfliers gaze at you curiously and smile as at a dead frog in a high school science lab as you are presented with the obligatory Gold Watch. They look like pallbearers awaiting the signal to lift your coffin from the rack and carry it to the graveyard. And the last elevator ride down to the street is the plunging ante-room to the greying out of all your days Or so it was back when a guy would get his foot in the door of some company and stay there his entire working life. Forty years or more with the same corporation.

That's how it happened with my grandfather, for instance. He managed to go from climbing poles on a line gang for the Chesapeake and Potomac Telephone Company in Martinsburg, West Virginia, to an office job in the state capital of Charleston with the same outfit. He retired at 65 and I am sure that within a week everyone had forgotten him. But he made it from the dirt road to the Office - and he was proud of that.

It's not like that now in our world of flex-time, hot-desking, and teleworking. Going from a small office shared with a group of other working stiffs to the ornate quarters of the Big Cheese was the dream of all the small fry in bygone eras. The door to the boss's office presented itself as an oceanic barrier between your world and his - like the difference between Purgatory (where you subsisted) and Heaven (his gilded domain). Women rarely saw the inside of those offices where the fluffy red carpet sprawled underfoot unless it was in the role of secretary. Which sometimes could be an ambiguous position...

Of course, the coronavirus has now caused a stampede *from* those offices, and it may be that remote working will empty the big centers almost completely. Anyhow, nobody stays in the same place or at the same job for very long. It used to be that if you had worked for three different companies in five years, the Grand Inquisitor at your latest job interview (there was no HR back then - another pleasant thing about the past - just "personnel') would take you for a fuck-up who couldn't hang around anywhere very long because of bad performance or bad breath. Now it's the norm, Covid or no Covid. The headhunters descend on talent like eagles on young bunny rabbits.

In truth, all the Covid virus has done is to close the doors of the physical offices and open virtual offices in our heads. Between these cerebral offices and the offices within the smartphone, it is no longer necessary to carpool it into the center of the mega-city or wait to sit or stand on crowded trains. So forget any notion of the extinction of offices. Oh no! It just means that the concept of an office has become smaller, smaller...and smaller. In the self-imposed paralysis of our special offices at home we can be everywhere and nowhere all at once. We hardly have to move a muscle.

What it means now is that we no longer need to pull on our suits or denims and actually *go* to the office. The office is buried inside us. The ancient Chinaman wouldn't have understood any of this. The look on his face would have been every bit as inscrutable as Caucasians always used to say about Asians'. But give him a week or two with us and he would be right on track. And he wouldn't miss the woman because she would be in her office right down the hall past the bathroom and bedroom.

Therefore, just as religion is adjusted to conform to the shape of our endless reconfigurations of God (jealous, vindictive, and punitive evolving into forgiving, loving, and merciful; mammoth overseer of the medieval world becoming the personal pal you can reach on your smartphone (in America especially where God is a shareholder) - so the idea of an office has changed to meet the alterations that life inevitably makes, generation after generation. The smoke-filled rooms of the past are mostly gone, replaced by easy-access cubicles in open space facilities where it is possible to see everyone milling about. Before the Virus, people were bringing their toys and teddy bears, frisbees and pillows, family photos, etc., and frequently one could expect to find hammocks and lofts and meditation rooms, and so on, in these office buildings - trying to make them less forbidding I suppose, and more as if a 'team' or 'family' really dwelt there instead of a bunch of corporate spiders angling for ever-higher webs. I hear they even took pictures of rats from the walls and that of the CEO glaring down from the ceiling like a blazing waffle iron.

In fact, I am in my office now. The dogs and car are nearby and the Boss is downstairs frying me an egg.

So maybe the very concept of 'office' - like drinking fountains, telephone booths, and airports/schools/football stadiums without massive security - is in the process of becoming an anachronism. To be replaced by the word r-e-m-o-t-e.

My father once owned a small airplane and when I visited him in New York City back in the 1960s, he took me flying over Manhattan. I remember that early morning when we floated across the city as the sun rose and the steam-filled mist was still draped around the tops of the buildings. The silver silence of those hours encased in the voluptuousness of reddening dawn and wan clouds of angels who had lost their way, made me think of the office cleaners who must still be inside. I imagined the New York city women running vacuum cleaners and emptying wastepaper baskets inside, and - strange me - I dreamed of finding some woman in there. Not a glamor girl, just a city girl of Irish or Puerto Rican descent. Or maybe Italian. Yes, a city girl finishing her nightlong shift on tired feet, those endless offices, that labyrinth in the sky. Rosie. Carmen. Chiara or Benedetta. But we flew on, and I never found her.

O, I was such a romantic.

So, I remember the words of that Chinese man who spoke all those centuries ago desiring only to finish the workday and go home to his love. When I taught English classes in Moscow,, I was happy when I sometimes went to 'Moscow City' - an array of expensive modern business centers -- and rode up high in one of the buildings that glittered in the dark evening - to give a language lesson. Though I prefer the old worlds of art museums, I confess to having grown to love those shiny, squirming buildings from which multitudes of people would flow at day's end to resume their stories somewhere else. And when I left at night, usually after a visit to the restroom and a quick but generous slug of the vodka I kept handy to make the long train ride home a bit more mellow, I would look back up at the still burning windows along their height and try to guess what was going on - what mysteries unfolding.

Odd that, because for the most part I knew the answer, having just been there myself. Nothing much at all was happening, yet it still seemed that life's important secrets could somehow be found out in those corridors and behind their doors. It made me want to go back and check.

Among the offices.

THE ENCHANTED RECYCLING OF OLD MOMS

I.

Two of my long-lost cousins in Florida have suddenly popped back into my life after an absence of well-nigh 13 years. That would be Arina and Matt. They are a welcome addition; they have rekindled old fires in my soul.

Actually, my deceased mom's sister (that I knew simply as Aunt Mary) produced four boys and a girl from a lousy small-town grotesque known to his drinking buddies as 'Herbie.' Mary used to say that she kept getting pregnant because it was the only time Herbie stopped beating the hell out of her.

I was a lot luckier than that. I was an only child. My dad caught the first bus out of town after I was born, but my mom and grandparents more than took up the slack.

At Christmas time, there were so many presents under the tree for me that I would trip over one while reaching out to grab the others. As I was heralded as a future Nobel Prize winner, my cousins may have felt a bit of resentment, though we often played together and got along fine.

I was smart at school, active in sports, and displayed all the predictable good boy etceteras one could hope for. It therefore came as a bit of a surprise when, at the age of 17, I climbed aboard the night-train to Hell, and didn't get off until about 40 years later.

Meanwhile, my poor super-efficient, nervous wreck of a mother, whose kindness and generosity to the whole family was rivaled only by her alcoholic knack of instigating aggravation and conflict, disappeared more and more often into a glass of bourbon as the years went by.

Sitting steadfast in her chair (I can see her clearly) like someone forever expecting the phone to ring with news of the death of the month, she was one of those neurotic people who will light a cigarette while there is still an active one smoldering in the ashtray. As a matter of fact, if you walked into her house and saw a curlicue of cigarette smoke snaking toward the ceiling, you knew that Mom was sitting directly under it.

My cousins, all of whom I maintained a relationship of one kind or another with for many years, were blessed with the gift of small-town wit and big city laughter. By which I mean that we thoroughly understood the petty and provincial meanness of life but enjoyed it as if it were something being performed on a Broadway stage. Whenever we got together, there was a lot of mirth, elbow bending, and profanity-on-parade.

You'd have thought we were sitting on the Board of Directors of some company and had just figured out a way to steal a million dollars from the share-holders. As I look back, I think we were strutting across a minefield and imagined we were heading for the hotdog stand on the 4th of July. That is to say, when everything started to explode, we thought it was still part of the celebration. Our city burned around us, and we laughed like hell and played our violins like a three-headed Nero. Maybe we were laughing so loud and hard just to scare the devils away. But the devils weren't scared. They were laughing too. So everyone was having a good time together: the murderers and those about to be murdered. A real love-in.

My two eldest cousins, Karl and Samuel, went different ways, but Arina, Matt, Tim, and I saw the signal given us by the Devil all dressed up in his immaculate clown costume, and when he wagged his finger and grinned his slobbering, unspeakably hateful grin, we bowed our heads and, for some reason, obediently followed.

Arina, the single girl in the group, was attractive, adorable, funny, spirited, and every bit as corruptible and promiscuous as any locker room guy soaping up for Saturday night. The two eldest avoided the alcohol and drug scene. The first-born, Karl, didn't look like he was headed for much, but he married a young lady (whom he later dumped) who pointed him in the right direction. He is a multi-millionaire now. A tycoon. And as mean as a sadistic undertaker.

The second, Samuel, became a first-rate plumber, and, for reasons known only to himself, decided to enlist as a half-a-redneck 'country boy.' He just up and disappeared into the Florida sticks. But Sam would later know tragedy when one of his teenage daughters took a shotgun and blew her brains out. There never was an answer to that one. I knew him least because, when he saw the booze-and-drugs carnage embarked upon by his younger siblings (with me as Master of Ceremonies), he politely excused himself.

Matt, the tallest and best looking - also the one with dark poetry in his heart - had become a master chef of the highest caliber. He had it all: the peach-pretty American wife, cute kids, the whole American enchilada. The good life. Then, after a painful operation for some neck injury (or so the story went) he discovered Oxycontin. (In America, it seems that if one drug doesn't get you, another one will.) The dope eventually put an end to all the tasty dinners he had once prepared on
cruise vessels.

In Dostoyevsky's *The Brothers Karamozov,* the oldest of the three is described by the author as being "wicked and sentimental." I wouldn't describe us that way; rather we were 'jovial and treacherous'.

Matt, upon losing the Chief Cook and Bottle Washer gig after passing out face down in his soup too many times, finally got into the medical business. The idea was to resurrect himself with a new career, but it wasn't such a good idea. Matt was a slick one, and soon was able to cop a bunch of Absorbine morphine pads, the kind hospice patients, for example, can clamp onto their arms or chest. The morphine will thus be drawn by the body heat of the afflicted into the bloodstream. It's an alternative to taking pills. Like blow-drying your ass instead of using toilet paper.

At his worst and nearly fatal point, Matt would take SEVERAL of these morphine pads and warm them up in the microwave. Then he'd smack them onto himself, sort of like a guy getting prepped in the electric chair and soak up the opiate sunshine. Nearly waxed him.

Arina ended up spilling more cocaine on the floor than most people ever put up their nose, and I became an alcoholic and crack addict. What a crew. That I somehow sandwiched a Ph.D. into the mix will forever remain one of life's mysteries. Not that it did me much good because by then I had a rap sheet.

But when we all got together at Christmas or the New Year we would put aside our woes and be jubilant. All of us but the Tycoon, who by this point had vaporized us from his thoughts and probably set about air-brushing us out of his family photographs. The Great Gatsby.

In our degraded state we never stopped laughing. To normal people this might seem an odd reaction to fucking up one's life, but maybe that's what pulled us through in the end. However, no matter how wild the party, no matter how raucous and prolonged, eventually the music fades and the fanfare fades and the tissue fades and the soul fades, and what you are left with the next morning is a pile of empty bottles and the only flash is that of self-hatred.

II.

My mom died on 6 September, 2006. Arina's mom passed (I was in Russia by then) on 4 February, 2014.

Arina who, just like me, couldn't seem to get well until after her mother left her, lives now with her hell-of-a-nice guy husband

Scott in Crescent City, Florida, near our old stomping ground of St. Augustine. She recently sent me some photos showing our two mothers as teenagers in Morgantown, West Virginia, their birthplace. I also remember a photograph I used to have of them when they were both members of the Morgantown High School band. My mom played the piccolo.

Seeing them in their salad years and heyday way back in the 1940s is enough to stop all traffic in my heart. It makes breathing difficult, as if some tubercular wind had blown through my soul. They look so safe in those photographs, sealed away from time and fate and death.

So looking a few days ago at some photos Arina sent me opened a narrow door through which I could stride into the past and see adolescent Jane (my mother) and Mary standing together in some old summer's backyard, their lithe, callow little arms and legs so squidgy liquid, like water shooting from a garden hose. Then my mind fast-forwarded to the last time I saw them: Mom as a dead body in a box and Aunt Mary as a crumpled and suffering old lady confined mostly to her chair - allowing me to view, holistically, I guess, the full circle of it all, the impassive but heartbreaking roundness of our seasonal lives - and it made me shiver inside, 70 years of blinking stone. Again it called for a clearing of the throat.

We weren't good to our moms. Alas, Not only "The Ariner" and me, but two of her brothers as well, became full-fledged, card-carrying poster boys and girl for the St. Augustine drink-and-drug culture. It's easy to fall into that there. St. Aug is a beach town full of honky-tonks, cabaret bars, cafes, trinket shops for the tourists, and no industry. What you get is a lot people in part-time or low-paying jobs: waitering-and-waitressing, working as tour guides for the mostly phony Spanish attractions (the city sells itself as being the oldest permanent settlement in America and the home of the Fountain of Youth. (Ironic, therefore, that it's where lots of people from up north retire to, grow
old, croak.)

If you've lost your driver's license because of too many DUI's, you can always give romantic horse-and-buggy rides to newlyweds in the secret alleyways of the town. Fuck that up and you can sell drugs or dust off your secondhand gee-tar and sing in the streets for beer money until the merchants and the cops run you off.

It's that kind of a place, although - as with most such quaint and picturesque little traps in Florida (and everywhere, I suppose), the tourists rarely see what a bunch of bums many of the locals, especially the young crowd, really are. And if you are there long enough, it is possible to witness the gradual decline of the maidens of the waves and the dunes - the Baywatch look-alike girls - as they lose their sultry, nubile sensuality, the goddess-grace their every step used to have as they padded like pornographic ballerinas along the sand - and so too many of them slowly disintegrate into alcohol-bloated coke hags with skin so beaten down by years absorbing the relentless sun that you could saddle a horse with their heavy, floppy flesh. Even their hands and feet have grown ugly by then - like ocean-stiffened shells - but mostly it's that brassy just-smelled-shit look etched into their hammered faces which tells me that the descent into real ugliness is a thing of the spirit as much as the flesh. The only thing that doesn't usually change is their nasty, in-your-face-asshole attitude.

The guys are no better. These ex-surfer dudes often end up looking like the jaded, half-crazy Vietnam war vets who used to come back from the rice paddies brain-wrecked and psychopathic. Part hippy, part redneck, long-haired and leathery, their discontented expressions look like they have just eaten a bad meal at a soup kitchen. Mariners who never went to sea, except maybe out on a few shrimp boats - they talk smack and do nothing. The town square, formerly known as the Slave Market (for obvious reasons) is always full in the early morning of homeless people sleeping rough in the grass and on the benches, like they are waiting for a bus which, like Godot, will never come. Greyhound refugees. Immigrants in their own country.

Arina, Matt, Tim, and I were the "Trainspotters" of St. Augustine at one point. In fact, since Tim was actually living in the woods for a lengthy spell, compassionate Arina used to drive around out in the boonies trying to find him lurking behind a tree and dump him off some beer and cigarettes. "Tim-spotting", she called it. Matt, the talented, well-paid and much-in-demand chef until he discovered Oxycontin, ended up with a brain aneurysm that damn near killed him. Flat-lined twice on the operating table apparently. But he retained a great sense of humor, as we all did. One of his favorite lines to describe himself was: "I've got a Mercedes in one arm and a Lamborghini in the other…and riding a bicycle." I, who had started university in 1967 and finally got my doctorate in 1997, was mowing lawns.

Our enabler moms supported us and the party went on and on. One of those "Hey, no harm in a few drinks" sort of thing. Then, like the clockwork of the comatose, it got worse without our really noticing. The quintessential downward spiral. DUI's, jail, court, probation, rehab, halfway houses, the lot. And, naturally, instead of legitimate soul-searching, our reaction to these supposed 'wake-up calls' was a stupendous binge to celebrate getting out of the cage. Trainspotters of St. Augustine.

Once or twice I landed a teaching job. In fact, at one point I had such a great part-time hustle at Daytona Beach Community College, and was so liked by everyone (I could still turn on the charm during my bright periods, but more importantly, I was good, for real), that they offered me a full-time job. I might still be in America if that had worked out. But whereas being a mere adjunct didn't require a background check, full-time work did. So I swallowed hard and hoped for a miracle and for a couple of months all was well. No word. Then the background check came back. Boy, THAT wiped the smiles off their fucking faces. You'd have thought they had seen a ghost. Fired. I've been fired more times than a Civil War cannon. But that time, if they had relied on my performance rather than a piece of paper, I might have turned it all around.

Typical of American hypocrisy in moral matters, they let me stay on for the rest of the semester because they knew if they ran me off too early I could sabotage them by burning the student roster where all the grades were inscribed. I could have given all my students A's, as in Absolutely Amazing, or F's, as in Fuck You's. Knowing this, they strung me along until the end, and as soon as I turned in my grades and office keys, they 'escorted' (frog marched) me physically from the campus. Like a Jew heading for Dachau.

So, I went to Europe and changed my life. (It's the story for another day.) But I'd no sooner got there than Mom fell and busted her hip for the second time. After her second husband died suddenly a mere week after his retirement (their golden years well-planned and stretching in front of them), Mom simply mixed herself into her Jim Beam and soda and never swam out. The first accident (she was drunk) was surmounted and she was good as new. But the second time (drunk again) left her an invalid because the doctors said her heart was too weak to survive the anesthetics required for the operation. She refused to go into a nursing home, so I bee-lined it back from Europe to take care of her. I had worked in old folks homes a lot, so I knew what to do. Arina used to come over a lot. I'd clean up Mom and give her meds and something to eat which she wouldn't touch. With no appetite, she just started to fade away. But I would do what I could. Then The Ariner and I would get fucked up. Addiction is a bitch.

One day, while we were watching a U.S. Open tennis match together (she was a great fan of Rafael Nadal), Mom just sort of hiccupped and died. She was in hospice and the way they work it, there are not supposed to be any 'heroic measures' taken. The terminally ill patient has already signed the document, and I guess if you happen to be sitting next to them when they start to go, instead of calling an ambulance you are just supposed to walk outside for a cigarette (two if you think the paroxysms are going to last a while) until it's over. But it's hard to do that if it's your mom, so I called the fire brigade and they said to put her on the floor and give her mouth-to-mouth until they got there.

I'll never forget that. It's one thing to wash your dying mother's genitals after she pisses and shits herself - it seems almost incestuous, certainly like a terrible invasion of her privacy. It's quite another to French kiss her after she is dead. But that's what I did. It didn't help, but at that moment there was no alternative. The medics got her heart started again, but they couldn't restart her brain. I called Aunt Mary. At the hospital, they put her on life support. Arina came with her mom, and when my Mom was doing her involuntary spasms, Mary hoped it was a sign of life. It wasn't.

Next came the travesty known as an American funeral. I was strung out and sleepless, but I had to make all the phone calls and attend to details.

Let's pause while I state my case about the funeral business. I believe that these simpering shit-asses represent the lowest point on the food chain. Funerals are terribly expensive, and, on top of that, the blood-suckers have made an art out of capitalizing on human grief. (They do it in Russia, too - the worst of the worst - and probably everywhere else this side of the nearest concentration camp, where they just load them in a ditch together free of charge.) The idea is that, although death may be the end of YOU, it is certainly not the end of Everyone Else. So somebody must clean up the mess and put things back together. Who else but the surviving family, assuming there is one? And since your family members are usually not serial jerk-offs who are prone to fling their dead aunties into manholes, dumpsters, or along the side of lonely country roads, the powers that be pounce like jackals on a dead rabbit to foist the financial responsibility of this clean-up job onto the survivors.

And then they start working on the guilt trip. It is the loving (maybe not, but obliged) family members' last chance to say goodbye and it is also society's last chance to rob the poor dead son of a bitch of his last nickel because, God or no God, after the carcass is twitching in the crematorium fire or starched out under the stony ground s/he is pretty much tapped out...unless, of course, there is more meat to be stripped from leftover credit cards and unpaid bills. So before the funeral home starts piping in the soft Death March Muzak with its caressing undertones, the sharks on the business end of it are still conniving for the last bite of the apple. And, like the IT industry, they are always adding new apps. In the case of Arina's mother, they were flogging videos. Film the ceremony and then watch it at halftime of the Super Bowl if you don't like the show.

Celebration of Life. In America, they don't mourn somebody's death anymore. They celebrate his/her life. I have nothing against this, but somehow it also seems like just another American way of avoiding reality. Because when all the symbolic balloons float away and the Life-Praisers go home, the bereaved widow, or widower is left alone with the Numbing Fact of Death. I have also noticed that, after yet another of America's mass murders takes place, be it at a school, shopping mall, concert, or wherever, they always have a 'candlelight vigil' to honor the dead. It was touching the first time or two; now it's obligatory - just another sideshow for the media. One of these days a mass murderer who is still at large is going to think to himself: "Damn, look at all those people standing there holding candles! Wonder how many I could take out with my SUV?"

In the United States, the cost of a respectable funeral is staggeringly exorbitant. Today, the average North American traditional funeral costs between $7,000 and $10,000. This price range includes the services at the funeral home, burial in a cemetery, and the installation of a headstone. While cremation is gaining in popularity, the traditional funeral is still the most popular manner for disposing of the deceased.

Here is a "ballpark estimate" of the main funeral costs. It's important to note that funeral prices vary considerably between funeral homes and geographic areas of the country.

- cost for a casket: $2,300
- embalming: $500
- cost for service in the funeral home: $1,000
- cost to dig the grave: $600
- cost for a graveling or outer burial container: $1,000
- cost of a headstone: $1,500
- fee for the funeral director's services: $1,500

In this example, total costs would approximate $9,000…and that's just for the "main" items. There could be additional charges for things like placing the obituary in the newspaper and buying flowers.

Knowing this, my mother had paid for all her funeral services in 1979. It was but one of her many farsighted decisions, as if, even then, she knew I would probably be out of pocket, and she was trying to save her own bones from the mice. Except, there was one oversight. For some reason, she forgot to account for the so-called "opening and shutting of the casket." In plain English, this means digging a hole, putting the body in it, and filling the hole back up again. It hadn't been paid for, and by 2006 inflation had raised the cost enormously. When she died, my modest chunk of change was tied up in her bank account because I had been spending more and more time abroad and wanted it to put myself in a position where I could not touch (blow) it.

When I returned from Russia to be at her side, I obtained Power of Attorney. But it was only good for as long as she lived; according to American law, Power of Attorney lapses at the moment of death. I couldn't get access to either her OR my money until the official Death Certificates made their rounds of four or five offices. Bureaucracy. That was going to take a week, and the funeral needed to be in three days. The gravediggers refused to dig the hole until they had their money. It was Florida and it was hot. I had no idea what sort of cadaver-slab or corpse-locker they were keeping her on or in (with, hopefully, a chunk of ice under it), but cooling systems in tropical locations don't always work, and I had visions of Mom starting to sweat in her cubicle. And rot. Meanwhile, I noticed that the magnificent casket that she had bought when times were good (caskets are richly ornate and very expensive; coffins are little boxes for the poor) lay open awaiting her meager little form, adequately stuffed by the taxidermist at the mortuary. What to do? Wheels turned in my exhausted, un-air-conditioned mind.

So I made a deal with the funeral director. "Put her in a slightly less expensive casket - but still a nice one (I emphasized !) - and the money that is saved can be diverted to the gravediggers, I mean the Openers and Shutters of the Casket. But remember, nothing tacky for my mom!" That is what I told him and he agreed.

The next day, which is when the mourners came to the funeral home to display their grief and view the ancient Barbie doll that the taxidermist, with help from the morgue hairdresser, had prepared, I saw at first what I expected: not my mom, but only a dead toy with one of those blank facial expressions which in a funeral parlor always looks more dead than Death itself. Wherever Jane Shumaker had gone, she sure as hell wasn't in that box. Her face was the color of powdered stucco, a mask spread over a skull filled with sawdust or turkey stuffing. But I do understand their predicament. A shit-eating grin would have been unseemly, and a savage, Fuck You All! grimace might have suggested that some sort of hell-bubble was already boiling beneath her. Therefore, like the basic concept behind all fast food, blandness of expression was the only choice.

Then I noticed what had really happened. I had come to the Death Salon expecting my mom to be resting comfortably in a slightly more modest but still attractive casket. Instead, the funeral director had put her in a plain little plywood receptacle like they used to bury heretics and murderers in and which now are reserved for the homeless. Mom looked like a stoned Olive Oyl from one of those Popeye the Sailor cartoons, and I was surprised that her spaghetti legs weren't dangling out over the edge. My Aunt Mary was waiting for me with apoplectic fury in her face. "How could you DO this to your mother that loved you so much!" she cried. "A pauper's grave for your dear MOTHER!!!" she shrieked. Aunt Mary thought I had traded in the casket and skimmed off the refund to fill my own pockets and go buy drugs. (I hadn't even thought of that neat trick.)

Anyway, my explanation fell on deaf ears, and, frankly, it WAS a disgrace. So I grabbed the funeral director by the scruff of his chinny chin-chin and, after the obligatory WTF ??? told him to put her in the original casket post haste. I used my mom's credit cards to pay everything off. Not strictly legal, but at that point, without sleep for three days, I just said (as I have been known to do) "Screw the Law." It was better than leaving my mom to linger until she turned into a glacier in a backroom freezer, or fester in a sweat-box at the storage unit until the formaldehyde wore off and her skin started sliding from her skeleton.

Everything went OK after that except for the graveside scene in the cemetery. I delivered the eulogy. My mom loved horse racing, and it so happened that the latest Triple Crown prospect and favorite had suffered a severe leg injury right out of the starting gate at the Belmont Stakes. So far the colt had survived the terrible injury, and I made the poetic analogy of comparing Mom to the horse. "The horse is still alive," I proclaimed, "and Mom would have wanted it that way!" The handful of mourners must have thought I was out of my fucking mind. Which I was. (The horse died the following week.) But it all made sense to me, and when, during the pastor's little talk, a cell phone went off while he was reading us a very solemn biblical passage, I nearly flipped. "Ta-Ra-Ra-BOOM-Dee-Day !!!!" it exploded like a celebration of some great moment in history, as if Washington had just crossed the Delaware and Lincoln freed the slaves all in the same moment. The only thing missing was the fireworks. And this jolly fuckery carried on for several seconds while the scandalized woman who had forgotten to switch off her phone frantically searched her big cavernous buttocks of a handbag for it. The sound effects made it sound as if my dead mother had just been named Woman of the Year by the chamber of commerce. Or perhaps launched on a rocket ship to the next galaxy.

I was too tired to make a scene. After all, it WAS my mom's funeral and I needed to be a good boy. So instead of paneling this hapless woman into the turf, I just put on my game face and stared straight ahead, tabulating that the sum total cost of this farce would have been enough to bail me out of jail maybe 35 times.

Or perhaps I spent those uncomfortable moments thinking about how I really would remember Mom. The answer? I recall her in that adjustable (you could crank the head up and down) hospital bed we had installed in the living room of her house so she could watch TV and pretend that she was still alive. I remember the innocent, sweet little girl aspect of her that the setting-in of a gentle dementia had produced. At midnight, she would arch herself up and smile at me as I sprawled on the couch, beer in hand. It was the mischievous, rather bewildered smile of one who is wandering in a big, flower-rich garden among friendly animals, or as if she and I both were co-conspirators in a harmless children's ruse, or playing a game like hide-and-seek or pin the tail on the donkey. I realized then that this fragile woman whose weak heart had once been so big and driven to a purpose, could no longer solve my problems.

She was my mother, but she was also my friend, and, even more, she was free of all regret, all animosity. She leaned against her pillows on that angled cot and smiled at me with truly angelic beatitude and charity. It was as if she hadn't even noticed my insufferable cruelty in response to all her kindness. And, now incontinent, she would thank me for helping her be dry of urine -

the way a blind man might thank the one who put out his eyes for at least walking him home afterwards.

III.

I sold the house and went back to Russia. I lost all contact with Arina and the rest of what was left of my family. I became a success. I turned it around. I had one marketable skill - the ability to teach English to foreigners — and in Russia they didn't care about background checks for Americans. My enabler was gone, so I enabled myself. In that awful, twisted, despicable sense, her death was her last and greatest gift to me.

Arina floundered for a while until her own mother died. Cousin Matt, the former great chef, stayed with her and took care of her the whole time. After she passed, the two rich cousins: Tim who had become successful in the air-conditioning business (after an initial financial boost from his wife), and Karl, the tycoon, turfed Matt out and basically commandeered Aunt Mary's car and house. In other words, they stole them. It should be said that one of these Good Samaritans, the tycoon, had long since found Jesus the Savior, and the other had discovered his Higher Power in Alcoholics Anonymous. Thus, while marching in the Army of the Lord, the essential asshole in them both came boiling to the surface.

Karl had been introduced to God after admiring the strength of his brother Sam at the funeral of his daughter who had, without any warning at all, committed suicide. At first Karl was under a pink cloud. He attended meetings of "Promise Keepers" (an organization devoted to guys who wished to be good husbands and family-men), and then he became a crusader in the "Warriors for Christ" movement, involving those Born Again stalwarts with their pikes upon their shoulders eager to do physical battle with the devil.

At first, he offered help to his drug and alcohol addicted cousins. Then he gave up. He decided that these people no longer deserved his beneficence. He bought mansion after mansion in many states, wherever the next promotion took him. Now he has one in Florida, of all places. No one knows why. The Promise Keeper, as it turns out, has his lady-loves on the side, and maybe the mansion is big enough to house them without the wife knowing. If she encounters them along the many corridors, she will think they are housekeepers. Housekeepers with diamond rings on their fingers and smirks on their lips.

Anyway, this gilded Promise Keeper showed up after nine years of no contact whatsoever with his mother to claim his share of the inheritance: $7000. A driblet more for the multi-millionaire. He came strutting in wearing a jewel-bedecked sheer white suit and sunglasses. He thought he was The Great Jablonsky. Arina said he looked more like Roy Orbison.

Basically, a Rhinestone Cowboy. And it had cost him a million to dress up like a Fool.

Fighting health problems and nothing guaranteed, Matt and Arina have fought their way back from oblivion. So have I. None of us knew we had the strength to do it, but we did.

Why couldn't we have done that, or at least started the journey, when our mothers were alive? Why couldn't we have made them proud of us when we had the chance? Why did their deaths release us? I don't have any idea. Maybe I had been spoiled but the others certainly hadn't.

Nor can I speak for them when I say that, despite my education and opportunities, there has always been a vagabond prowling and rummaging through my spirit. If I see a tramp on the street, I don't turn blind all of a sudden or think to curse him. I shudder because I recognize him.

Once when I was driving the car up to Jacksonville to spend time with a crack-whore I knew, I was drinking beer to get in the mood, and then I started glancing up at the rear view mirror. I started smiling, then grinning, as I saw the transformation taking shape in my face. Eric the Professor changing into a werewolf right before his own eyes, right there on I-95.

Maybe they loved us too much. We thought, or must have thought, that they were immortals in mortal form who would support us forever and never leave us. We could go on being Trainspotters of St. Augustine forever. We could not accept that they were growing frail; it did not dawn on us how we were slowly killing them - as well as ourselves - every time we did stupid things. We thought they would live forever, and maybe come to OUR funerals.

We were wrong.

You know, maybe we shouldn't make too much out of people like Arina and Matt and me who finally sort themselves out. The people who have been 'sorted out' from the beginning must sneer at this. At best, they might finally say, "Thanks for FINALLY getting it right (you fucking idiots)," but they will always, most of them, feel contempt and have a sense of being better. Just like Roy Orbison, our brother and cousin, who, at this very moment is likely sitting in his mansion of many vast and empty rooms.

Just for the record, Matt met a lovely Hispanic girl with a voluptuous soul and a big, expressive, joyful family, and now lives in a different city. I am sure he still remembers many of his old recipes - to their delight, no doubt. Arina has some health issues, but she has lasted long enough to learn to accept life on life's terms. She has a good husband. They love each other, but - perhaps just as importantly - they like each other. I would call that spiritual.

No, I haven't darkened the doors of a church for a long time, but I find this miracle-laden mystery that we call life most compelling. I have no answers, but it is hard to escape the notion that our mothers left something of themselves behind for us that was far more valuable than money. Maybe they walk inside us.

Maybe that's why we have gotten better. I wouldn't put it past the old gals. They weren't perfect by a long shot, but they were good people. We were bad children while they were alive and we should have reached out to them as they reached out to us. We didn't, except for drunken protestations of love that, in those, days, was purely counterfeit money.

Now we are better. We are whole. Do they know it? Well, I wouldn't venture a guess as to that, because I have no idea if they do or if they don't. The cosmos works in mysterious ways. But, speaking only for myself, it feels like something good must have been recycled and fed to me just when I needed it most.

I lived in Russia for ten years. Now Bulgaria. I will probably never go back to the United States. There's no reason. Mom's bones are there, true. People would point me to the Evergreen Cemetery in St. Augustine, Florida, and say, "She's right out there. Over yonder. Go right, then left, then right again, and you'll come to the plot. She's right there."

No, she ain't. Ah, the recycling of old mothers.

I have noticed lately that in my dreams and twice-daily sojourns with my trusty dogs, I see Mom's face and hear her voice. My grandparents often join her, and I have even noticed my dad once or twice. He died last year at the age of 90. Rather strange, don't you think that, as the past just gets farther and farther away, they start to come nearer? Around their feet are some of my favorite old dogs, too. They come closer. And all of their voices seem to be getting louder. As loud as car horns sometimes.

Is it for a reason?

I will ask Arina and Matt. They won't know either, but we can discuss it. Just a trio of orphans laughing like hell and wiping tears from their eyes. Ghosts are laughing with us.

THE SILENCE AND THE DARKNESS

I remember being afraid of the dark when I was a kid. I lived in a tumbling old alabaster house at the end of a street that ran its course and then collapsed into sinking woods. We were way up in the hills. I slept in an upstairs room, and I always thought that lunatics with chainsaws might climb up the side of the house and that zombies with hideous intentions were hiding in the closet. The fear was real, but it was based on a dread of *contact*, the proximity of evil companions beyond all comprehension.

Sitting up under blankets late at night, hyper with the total paranoia of an insect in a reptile-infested swamp, I would survey the darkness for sudden, subtle movement. I was rather frail as a child, often sick and nightmare prone. The darkness would eat me, and I knew it. Sometimes I would go sit in the bathroom and turn on the light and lock myself in. This was better than death.

It was a long time ago.

I grew up and reached college age in a time when it was cool, trendy, and relatively safe for young long-haired people to hitchhike up and down and across the country. (Yes, young women, too - can you imagine doing that in America now?) This was before the psychopaths got wise to it and started claiming the highways for themselves, leaving dead, mutilated hitchhiker bodies in their wake.

We had romantic notions - a 1960's recycling of that old, marvelous American urge to ride the rails or join the circus - 49ers and Sooners all of us at heart - and this seemed a great way to discover our nation from its roots, from the ground floor up. And it could be heaven if a van full of hippies picked you up. If it was your personal sunny day from the God of Light, you might even find yourself in the back of the van exchanging 'intimate pleasantries' with one of those earth-mother girls who would seem anachronistic now but who, back then, could cast a spell like some old Celtic ballad - and getting so stoned that when they dropped you off you thought you were in Mexico. Yeah, it was really like that back in the '60's. Even now, the words of the old Simon and Garfunkel song ring in my ears: "Counting the cars on the New Jersey Turnpike, they've all come to *look for* America (my italics)." Fantastic song.

An evening came when my thumb had taken me somewhere out of the way, and the driver had dropped me off near a crossroad saying he was headed in a different direction. He told me to follow the asphalt down to the ribbon of two-lane blacktop below and try to catch a ride there. He added the cautionary note that it was not a busy road and that I might need to wait a while before anyone came along.

It was perhaps prophetic that, just as I was descending the ramp, the only streetlamp nearby went flickering out. The clouds above had gathered in the darkness like a somber committee, consuming all traces of the moon and stars, and it was really difficult to see anything. At all. The wind had picked up and it took my last matches to light a cigarette. It must have been my final cigarette too, because when it was done, there was nothing.

All of a sudden, I became aware of myself being swallowed up in what I can only describe as a vast Cosmic Sensory Deprivation Unit. I felt as though I had awakened alive in the stark middle of my own death. Nothing had ever been blacker, more devoid of connection, equilibrium, direction. It was utterly unnerving... Not at all like wandering through a graveyard or even a forest at night, imagining the breath of murderers and goblins. No, under the circumstances, the company of a killer would have been a relief, something to struggle with. When the foe is Nothingness and all of your hooks and handles are gone, then you realize how terrifying the God you have abused all your life might really be.

It was like deep space. Darkness beyond darkness. Silence beyond Silence. Back then I guess the moon landing had already occurred, the 'space race' with the Soviets was in full swing and there was plenty of talk about astronauts and cosmonauts. The potentially horrible fate of some (imaginary) astronaut (Me) who had gone outside the space capsule, lost his grip on the safety rope, and just started drifting helplessly out into space...to die out there...had come to my mind frequently.

The worst death. Worse than cancer or being greased by an 18-wheeler or mauled by a tiger. Worse than mafia guys chopping you up with an ax. Just drifting, the tiny human computer we call our brain flashing and throbbing like a little radio somehow inexplicably forgotten on an abandoned stone in the middle of nowhere, wailing at nothingness or shouting the evening news to the massive indifference of eternity...

Why did I think it was so terrible? Maybe it was because of the sense of ultimate excommunication, of gazing down at the earth (I the suddenly lost astronaut) and understanding that, even as you sort of presided over it, you were no longer part of it and never would be again. They weren't listening, that earth of strangers. And you could see once and for all that the stars, what stars there were, were no more receptive to you than the exotic birds of a tropical island if you had been marooned there without other people. The bright stars were all dead to you and the earth was sailing away with its other lives, and there you were. Floating amid nothingness...and with nothing to do but think, think, think, until, like breath itself, all thoughts left you and you died.

Nightmare. And that is exactly how I felt on that road of invincible blackness.

Of course, a car came eventually, and I went surging back into the mainstream. But I have never forgotten the experience of Death-in-Life that I had out on that road.

Now, interestingly enough, I find myself half-longing to enter such Silent Annihilation again. I am not speaking of death-wish, or, if so, it is subliminal and not based on any willful or even flickering, impulse-based desire to die, like when you stand on a high balcony and clutch the railing. Maybe it's that where I once found terror, now something in me, some unknown mechanism which the years have aroused from hibernation, speaks to me about the Peace that is found in Darkness and Silence.

And perhaps it has something to do with the fact that, having lived for years in cities such as Moscow, Rome, and London (and even in various minor burghs of the modern world) where it never gets dark - where there is always artificial light after the daylight is gone, and almost always the pulsations of human-manufactured *noise* - now I live in a distant village where I walk my dogs at 5.30 a.m. in the dark and then sit on my balcony facing the valley and the forest, watching the sun rise up out of the sea on the other side of the mountain and the winged flocks gliding through the untouchable fabric of the silken wind of the sky's soul.

It's different every morning, just as the evenings are different when the dogs and I climb the hills and, when the ground isn't besotted with lumpy mud from the winter rains, wander out to where a long line of telephone poles connected by electric wires such as guide the trolley buses in old European cities gradually disappear into the primordial mist. I imagine how a million conversations must be streaming pell-mell along the tiny autobahn inside those rope-like wires, but the dogs and I hear only the silence.

At such times I understand how this globe of human life - and the discordant strains of its raucous parade, always somehow distant to my ears - burns and refuels, flowers and festers, poised like an aneurysm that could explode at any moment - or a water bubble that might evaporate - suspended in a sky that is not really a sky, but only an ever-expanding (and throbbing) pretend-dome, an idiot-box full of flaming ball-bearings all millions of light years apart...of many silences, reaching out to greater and greater Silence and more and more Darkness...until nothing is even throbbing anymore, not the silence, not the darkness, only a void within a void within a void, and nowhere to be found a solitary cymbal smash of a single blink of an eye. Stillness. When I stand in that place in the embrace of the mist watching the telephone poles disappear like a succession of dead relatives, I do not know if I am happy or sad. If happy, it must be because I feel I am in the presence of something always yearned for but never found, some life never lived. And if I am sad, it is for the same reason, with the added anguish that I know I will *never* find it now; that my life was like some passionate, all-day fox hunt rich in wind and color, but the fox was just a ghost. There never was a fox, and, as I realize this and look back, I see that all my companions, all those horsemen and women, are gone too. I understand with a shudder that they also were only ghosts and now I am left alone among the stony and brooding juries of the deep forest, dense trees that never say Innocent or Guilty, but just leave one to wonder forever and ever, as now evening with its sempiternal stillness comes.

As I am late in life and have lived among the cities, I am used to noise. It is inevitable and I understand this, but so much is just an invasion. For example, everywhere I have ever gone in Europe and Russia - I mean to cafes, fitness centers, restaurants, etc., what do I hear? Noise. Music I don't want. It is ALWAYS piped in American/British racket from a different pop era, and most often junk I didn't like the first time it offended my ears. Imagine my take 40 years later. But I am forced to accept it. And when I walk the streets of cities, I hear everyone chattering on their phones, eyes goring into the gadgets that consume them and demand their fealty. I want to tell these people, STOP: listen to silence. Listen to the universe. And if they said, Sir, what should we listen for? I would have to reply that I didn't know. Should I say, Nothingness? Wow, what a selling point.

When I used to work in nursing homes in Florida, I handled a lot of worn-out people whose bodies were turning back into dust and ash before my very eyes. In many cases, the brains were malfunctioning, too, and there were days and nights I looked into eyes that were wide open but did not look back at me. Zombie eyes, terrified, plane-crash eyes. But I also met indomitable types whose insatiable spirits had outlasted their bodies, and who, on the brink of midnight, or at 2 a.m., when I changed their sheets and wiped away their incontinence, would still open themselves to me and say good night, and talk with blazing clarity, as well as with softness and circumspection. Wise individuals who were not intimidated at all by the fact that their bodies were dying around them. O what lovely people! And when I would check in, late at night and see them sleeping, their thoughts buried deep inside their decrepit, fading flesh-capsules, I would imagine them in the middle of some dream, still chasing rabbits, still in love, still preparing for war. And I knew, I sensed it, that they had gone away for the night to a better place, and furthermore a place of their choosing, where death was just a joke to be talked about later, after the absinthe and the sex, and next morning's hangover among rainy streets. Furtherance of life. They were in a Twilight Kingdom.

I understand all of that now. The ineffable beauty of silence when the spirit is telling you a wonderful tale. But I know I would have needed to be inside their broken bodies, running through the avenues and alleys of their brains, to hear
their stories.

If you have ever seen a battlefield (as I have only on film) when the war is over and the scores of dead bodies are lying everywhere, you can appreciate the profound silence leftover from where life *was*. Only the ripple of a breeze now. If you actually walk on such a battlefield, as I have at Gettysburg and in Greensboro, North Carolina, you can still hear the soldiers.

If you are at Stonehenge and listen to the wind, you can hear the Druids at work, their throaty cries coming from a Deep Web in the back of your mind. I suppose this is what Jung meant by the Collective Unconscious.

If you go to Pompeii, as I have several times, and walk among those grid streets, you will understand that the people of two thousand years ago have just abandoned the bartering and sensual clamor of the ancient morning, and now have disappeared from the shops and markets for their siesta. No doubt, some of them, behind closed doors, are making love. And you know that if you wait, just until evening, they will come out again and join you in the streets.

Maybe this is what William Blake meant when he wrote the following: "To see a World in a Grain of Sand/And a Heaven in a Wild Flower/Hold Infinity in the palm of your hand/And Eternity in an hour."

I wonder what those old monks were thinking centuries ago when they lived in mountain crags and made cells for fasting and prayer out of small dents in the sides of cliffs. So, for me - after years and years of chasing the sounds of accordions along city streets, searching for women who would smile back at me as they climbed the stairs; after the tumultuous stadiums where great games were played; after all the morning and evening rush hours where dirty, delicious, endlessly seductive humanity poured itself out to me - all there for the taking - now I find myself retreating into mental monasteries.

Someone is playing Eric Satie's "Gymnopedie №1" on a distant piano, and the melody, infinitely pure, infinitely haunting, allows me to finally live the lives I never lived.

THAT RASPBERRY FACE

I can remember my undergraduate days more than a half century ago and sitting with friends until the wee hours having philosophical discussions about things like 'God.' The memory grows fuzzy, but it seems to me that we gave God at least a 50-50 chance of existing. Maybe, mixed in with the residue of an upbringing that took the reality of Heaven and Hell for granted, we were still hedging our bets and wondering out loud: "Well, what does He expect of us?" (God was a 'He' back then.) Not "How can we *serve* 'God'?" - but "Where in the hell's half-acre is He, and what does He want?"

Those were the candle-lit years before technology; therefore, such conversations actually occurred face-to-face amid real, flesh-bearing people. The sharpest pupils of life among us had been introduced to Nietzsche and Kierkegaard, Sartre and Camus. Existentialism and Life as Absurdity did not sound very fetching to me, so probably at that point I was still, deep-down, rooting for God...

I also read *Waiting for Godot* and Eugene O'Neill's haunting play *The Iceman Cometh,* and as the years rolled by, I found myself in the same exasperating state of waiting for a confirmation that never came. "Just *one* damned miracle," I would mutter. "Is it too much to ask?"

I didn't need to see the Red Sea part, I didn't need to see my great grandmother come back from the dead, farting out the formaldehyde as she shook off the stench of the coffin and blinked away the cobwebs of death tilting and swaying in her eyes. (Let it be said, however, that I *would* have settled for some water turning into wine.)

On Sunday mornings back then, the television was flooded with religious programs, and those included more than one
Faith Healer.

Some cripple would be wheeled in and tossed up on a gurney, and the evangelist would go to work, panting, pumping his arms until circles of sweat appeared in the pits, shouting and shrieking, and (in the case of Oral Roberts, one of the big boys in the faith-healing business), the punch line would come when he placed his hands on the legs of the lame supplicant and cried out H---E---A----L !!!! at the top of his lungs, and the guy would jump off the gurney like a leprechaun and start dancing a jig. Naturally the audience would go crazy, swooning at the undeniable presence of the Lord Himself right here in the TV studio.

It was almost better than Professional Wrestling. But it proved nothing to me.

It wasn't even that I expected such a dramatic event as Death-into-Life to put things right for me. As I 'matured', I began merely to hope for some kind of luminous epiphany, a Road to Damascus experience, as if some magic spell or hypnotic trance would come over me, and all my doubts would vanish.

I wanted to walk into the forest one day as an atheist and come out the other side a Believer. And it wouldn't have mattered a jot what had happened in the forest to bring this about. Just the result.

As time wore on, and my life waxed and waned from ripeness to rot, I began to hate God. Whereas before I would have called myself an 'Agnostic', now I would savagely splutter that I was an "Atheist." But here is where the word 'absurdity' could really be applied in a meaningful way. For if I was an atheist, then I didn't believe God existed; yet, if I hated God, was that not an admission, albeit in an ass-backwards kind of way, of *faith*?

Why did I hate God? The Great Theologians of past and present could, of course, present arguments that would make my conclusions look like those of a child about to have a tantrum.

But I based it on two things:(1) The *Unfairness* of Life; (2) The *Unhappiness* of Life.

I guess I was hardly the first guy to look around at all the misery and ask, "How could a Loving God permit this?"

Of course, there were happy moments: pizza and football, beer and sex. But Nobody came from the sky or from out of a tree trunk to rescue the little girl abducted and butchered by the pedophile. No Holy Hands with gentle palms reached out to save the crashing jetliner and all those aboard.

The Savior was always Out to Lunch.

Or maybe it was not Christianity as a concept that I disliked as much as I despised 'practicing' Christians themselves. I recounted the many atrocities committed in the name of the God of Love, and every time I heard some 'Born Again' Christian howling on the street corner - they grow like weeds in America and, prior to their conversion, most often were dedicated assholes of the first rank who thought they'd now stumbled upon an easy and painless way to wash off the sins of decades, and jump the queue of the gateway to heaven), my blood would start to boil afresh.

And after hearing all the Great Arguments of all the Great Theologians, I still feel this way.

True, as I start to age precipitously and hourglass drains, I feel a genuine and growing presence inside me. Yes, indeed. But, alas, it's not the presence of God. It is the presence of Death. God now stands at the outermost periphery of all my excruciating inner conversations and sermons to myself. I say: "Maybe I am overlooking something. Maybe there is something staring me straight in the face that I am missing." But it's death that I feel in my bones, slowly hollowing them out into tunnels of
odorless emptiness.

Nor do It feel as though anything is coming to my rescue. I think to go the way of the little girl abducted from her play and the plummeting aircraft until I reach a point beyond all pain.

For all of that, however, there remains something at the deepest core in me, deeper even than the marrow of the bones - maybe an intuition that won't be obliterated. Perhaps I hear the distant crashing of some Jungian river of archetypes whose swirling fury hisses at me like primordial insanity. A *hunch* embedded like the innermost circular grains in the center of huge trees.

There seems to be something - I don't know what it is - which tells me that all will be well, that things will be fine at the end of all endings. I get this feeling now and then. I don't know what to call it, or whether to trust it, or where it is coming from, but it catches me like a gale-force wind battering a, swaying sky-scraper, then, after it dies down a little, like a zephyr at dusk amid rows of corn whose endless distances beckon, beckon, beckon...

So I never know if this drop of faith, like a naked hermit in a blizzard or a snowflake in a ball of fire, is based on things real or unreal. But I can never completely...blot it out.

This morning I was having one of my terrific conversations with Yasha, the art director who is my student and friend. We discussed the future of Art in terms of Artificial Intelligence. This came about after I had shown her an article that forecasts the coming time (soon) when human beings will begin to have deeply intimate relationships with robots. Sex included, followed or preceded (as the case may be) by deepening love. We will wed our robots.

It's going to happen; there is no way to avoid it. In fact, I'd say it will provide a wonderful alternative for people who, for various and sundry reasons, cannot find or sustain such relationships with real people. Already, books (fiction and nonfiction) have been written on this subject. I even wrote a short story on the theme myself.

According to Yasha, computers can now generate art, music, and poetry which, while not yet at the level of Renoir or Chopin or Yeats, are nevertheless acceptable as offerings on the level of a rather dully mechanical but arguably legitimate 'artist'. Who knows where it might lead?

Some years ago, when photography was invented, it looked like all the painters would go out of business. Who would need some guy to spend days smearing oils into the form of a portrait or landscape when the camera could produce a perfect likeness? (For example, who uses typewriters, phone booths, or encyclopedias today?)

So the artists knew they had to come up with something, and one of the things they came up with is what we now call 'Impressionism'. Evidently, there is an 'artistic impulse' in human beings which technology cannot entirely dominate or stamp out. Or is there?

My wife has taken up painting, and I see that she possesses a talent for it, a natural blessing of eye and hand, and a happy coordination between them both. Plus a strange and fertile imagination. We were walking our dogs the other day, and as we approached the forest and the skyline above it, I explained to her about how people like Monet were, in effect, painting *light*. How they would stand in the fields all day (Van Gogh with his flask of absinthe under the blistering sun) and paint, paint, paint, trying to capture the light as it inexorably changed from one hue to another - subtle, decisive. The cameras of the day couldn't capture that.

Yasha suggested that if you set up a computerized camera in a field and instructed it to take a photo every single second, and at the end of the day some robot or art critic with limitless stamina combed through every one of those 86,400 images (for that's the number of seconds in a day), they would be sure to find several that could be called 'masterpieces.'

It appears to be, as they say, the 'wave of the future' - never mind that neither Google nor Yandex can adequately translate a poem or even an idiom or piece of slang without disaster or comedy taking place.

Nevertheless, one day the computers will simply gobble up all the human beings. Count on it. Or think of it this way: the dinosaurs died out 65,000,000 years ago. Before that, it is estimated that they dominated the earth for about 165,000,000 years? Quite a chunk of time, I would say. Human beings have been around for about 200,000 years. Things changed slowly at first, then faster, then faster and faster, and now in the blink of an eye. If the human race somehow survives for another million years, how should we begin to imagine the outcome? My guess is that the human race *as we know it* will have long since ceased to exist. They will have disappeared into their machines, and those machines will have disappeared into others even more unimaginable.

I call it evolution. Monkey into Man, Man into Machine, Machine into Who Knows What? A natural process. What is so strange about it?

Did the 'ancient' Romans go around calling themselves 'The Ancient Romans'? Heck, no; the children of the Roman Empire represented the 'cutting edge', 'state of the art' country club of the world back then. They were the Hot Shots of the Mediterranean and Adriatic. Now they are the 'ancient' Romans. As one day *we* will be the ancient world. Bill Gates and Elon Musk will be regarded the same way we think of Socrates and Aristotle.

Ultimately, civilization will be a matter of Machines cohabitating with Machines. So, given all these remarkable developments, God has sort of gotten lost in the shuffle.

Still, I remember one summer day about 15 years ago in Daytona Beach, Florida. I had just gotten out of jail and was living in a halfway house. We had to work as part of the Probation Game, and so I had a job at McDonalds. I spent the summer flipping burgers. One day I had knocked off and gone for a stroll along the beach. There was an outdoor establishment where they were selling hot dogs and soft drinks and stuff, and I went in and took a seat. Just sat there soaking up the heat of the day.

All of a sudden, a little girl burst in with her Mom. She was carrying several vividly-colored balloons, and her face was generously painted over with some sort of raspberry concoction she had been licking, most of which seemed to have missed her mouth and found her nose and cheeks. Her countenance was just a raspberry mess!!! A smorgasbord of merry smears of cherry berries!

But what has stayed with me all these years was her expression, that wild, giddy look her eyes had when she swept in with her balloons. It was an expression of unshackled, boundless, absolute, infinite *Joy.*

No darkness around the edges. No second guessing. Nothing hesitating in her peerless little eyes. *Happiness.*

And I distinctly remember registering a single thought: Either this means Nothing, or it means Everything.

No in-betweens. In-between was impossible. Nothing.
Or Everything.

One roll of the dice against an overwhelming vastness whose silence cries Nothing! Nothing! Nothing!

Maybe I'm a fool, but I decided, against all odds and everything life on earth has beaten into me, that what throbbed in her reddening smile meant EVERYTHING.

3.

THE SUMMERS OF MY WINTER AFTERNOONS

THE VALLEY OF THE SHADOW OF DEATH

Tonight, I watched a video of a young Chinese daredevil falling to his death from the 72nd floor of some building in China. He put himself there, on top of that great building, for reasons as complex as the human brain and as bleak as the human heart, but if it had been possible to ask him why, he probably would have had nothing remotely interesting to say about it.

"Uh...adrenaline rush."

There he was, alone (whoever was filming him from a distant window will forever remain anonymous to me), except for the other skyscrapers sticking up around him. There was no dramatic view of whatever lay far below (mostly asphalt, one assumes), which made it unlike some of the other daredevil and bungee jumping videos I have caught from time to time, which are usually filmed in exotic locations.

So maybe it was the silence and barrenness of detail which created the effect of a ritualistic yielding to emptiness. Just the black and white recording of his at first methodical movements as he prepared to lower himself from the roof and let his body dangle against the side. One felt his isolation. I knew what was going to happen. I was drinking tea, pawing at a sandwich. It made me nervous. Why didn't I turn it off?

He begins confidently, fooling around at the great height, then, having - I guess - assessed everything he thought important, lowers himself over the edge. His head moves back and forth. Suddenly he does three chin-ups. The party piece. Then he straightens his legs and rests for a moment. Next, he tries to climb back up but it doesn't work. His shoes refuse to grip. No doubt that's what he was counting on. That the shoes would grip the long high facade-wall of the building peak and he could simply thrust himself back up.

But there is no grip. At what point, at what cataclysmic instant, does his brain register this? That it won't work?

Was he ready for that sudden, crumpling, blackening, vomiting nausea that surely swept through his brain?

He turns, apparently as a last resort, his body sideways. Then back. He hangs there, two thin strands of arms that are already dying because they are tired and resist what his brain must by now be shouting at them. All to no avail. In two or three seconds, he releases his grip - or his grip releases him - and he disengages from the building. Falls. Disappears from sight.

As this is happening, I think (I truly believe) that I am experiencing - as if the same electrodes were attached to both of us - something of what he knows now. Because I feel vertigo and sickness.

Then, which I am ashamed of...I watched the whole thing again. I invited myself to experience again a kind of 'virtual' death in the form of attaching myself, like a parasite, to the annihilation-experience of another person.

It's like, on those rare occasions when I go to the zoo, I enjoy the monkeys, giraffes, and polar bears, but I can't wait to get to the reptile section. And when I am there, imagine myself being bitten by one of those deadly snakes. I think about the sharp pain caused by their rapier teeth (two ghastly needles) and feel the poison draining into me. I imagine the tremor, like drinking a high potency energy drink too quickly. But I never imagine it happening in a crowded place where someone can rush to my rescue. No, it's always in some remote part of Australia or Africa where there is no help. My dread of the lethal snake increases the terrible beauty of the nightmare.

Maybe it is like wanting to meet Death just to find out if "IT" is really as bad as all that. I am sure that men (and women) on Death Row in the world's prisons are divided between wanting to hang on to life as long as possible - even if it means just one more cigarette please before we go - as they are being led to the place of execution — and also being fascinated by the prospect of knowing, really knowing... What. It. Is. Like.

I knew a young woman who committed suicide in 1981 while I was attending the University of Florida. Her name was Robin Baldwin and she was in the creative writing program. She was beautiful and friendly, but somehow not together, always late for everything, always in a kind of upheaval. She always wore bandages around her ankles.

Once I had an English friend who was in the British Royal Navy visit me while his ship was docked in Jacksonville. He met Robin, who at that time was renting a room in some woman's house. We were going to a bar and we stopped by the house for her to pick up something she needed. Tim and I waited and waited in the car, and finally I just went in. I will never forget the state of her room, nothing I have ever seen from a woman certainly. It was an utter wreck, total chaos, a nightmare. To this day I believe that this room was a perfect representation of that poor lovely woman's mind. A year later she stayed with my girlfriend and me in our apartment. She had gained a lot of weight. But it wasn't the weight, it was the distance between hanging on and giving up that somehow seemed to express itself. She had left her body, like a horse slipping his halter and running away in the far-off moor.

Then one morning I read a headline in *The Gainesville Sun*. In the 'Police Report" section, I saw a headline: "University Student Leaps to Her Death." I knew it was her. And it was. She had jumped from the 7th floor of the Psychiatric Unit of the University Hospital. I later found out that she had tried it before and survived. She had damaged her ankles, and that was why she kept them wrapped.

During my time at Florida State some years later, I had a female student who also thought about suicide. I was teaching then, and she was in my English class. I had my students keep a journal. They could write about anything. This girl wrote about her intention to commit suicide. I guess a lot of people, including me, have thought about taking this route before. It is hard for me to suppress a very inappropriate smirk when I read that someone has attempted suicide x-numbers of times. I always have this sinister sense of humor that wants to ask them: "What's the problem? Did you ever think of just stepping out in front of an onrushing bus? Or…leaping from the 62nd floor of a building in China, for example? Trust me, it will work!"

Very bad of me. But from this young woman's journal entries, I decided she wasn't kidding. Like the film of the Chinese boy, there was a coldness, an emptiness, a sort of emotional vacuum there — a kind of Nothingness. And that told me she was serious. I reported it and got her help. I don't have any idea what became of her.

I think that many people would like to be dead without going through the actual process of dying. This applies to anyone who ever went to sleep in a fit of despair and hoped that they wouldn't wake up. That God would do the dirty work… quietly, unobtrusively, like locusts destroying a tree, tons of plastic killing a sea, or a recuse spider hatching its eggs in the deep recesses of your arm or leg. But I also happen to believe that most teenagers who commit suicide are merely play-acting. They want to punish the living and then theatrically accept their apologies when they come back to life. They don't recognize the finality involved. Nobody is going to welcome them back with a note saying "S-o-r-r-y about not Dancing with you at the Prom!" and a bouquet of flowers.

There was a film that came out in 1981 which was called *Whose Life Is it, Anyway?* The story is about a 32-year old sculptor named Ken Harrison who is seen at the beginning of the film wrapping up a jovial, productive day with his students at a Boston art institute. His rapport with them and his vital, brightening energy are obvious as he jumps into his car and drives off for what we have no doubt will be a full-tilt weekend of creativity and love. But he never gets there, Instead, he is involved in a terrible accident. He tries to laugh it off as they slide him into the ambulance, but later he is informed that he is paralyzed from the neck down: a quadriplegic. At the appropriate moment, the doctors solemnly explain the facts to him.

So, the film becomes a study of Harrison's ultimate choice to have his reluctant physicians switch off the machine that is keeping him alive, and therefore to die. It is painful to watch, especially when he verbally abuses his girlfriend (a dancer, ironically) and shoos her away so that she may restart her life without him. He is being kind.

One of the main themes of the film has to do with the intense legal battles that have to be fought before Harrison is allowed to have his decision carried out. Does the patient have the right to die in this manner or are the doctors ethically/legally obliged to keep him ticking as long as possible in order to please God and be able to say to one and all that they did everything they could?

The final scene shows Ken Harrison finally alone, finally left alone, in his hospital room with the machine significantly No Longer Buzzing. We study his face as the film ends. Dismally steadfast. Intact, even though, like the particles in one of those science labs I used to be assigned to in high school where one inlay was superimposed over another, we can see it cracking up underneath. It reminds me a lot of the loneliness, the final estrangement, of that Chinese boy dangling from the ledge, suspended over the abyss.

I remember when my family first brought me to Florida back in 1967. I hated the place the second I saw it: steamy April after coming down from frosty St. Paul, Minnesota. Moving into a one-story house, smeared with dull pastels. Anyway…we of course went to the beach a lot. I liked bodysurfing, which means just going out as far as is reasonable and then catching a wave to ride back in on. Believe me, it doesn't amount to much - not like really surfing, which I didn't want - but it's a beer drinker's way of swallowing a lot of salt water and getting an ocean tan.

One day I strayed out too far. If you haven't been near the ocean you won't understand. But the ocean has its own rules, and one of them is that the water comes in over the top and goes out at the bottom. They call it a riptide when it really gets funky, and what it means is that you can be standing in shallow water one minute and flushed out into the VERY deep end the next - swept out to sea. There are lifeguards on hand, but they can't watch everything all the time, and people get in trouble like this and some of them drown. It's like in the Grand Canyon. You can try to keep tourists from falling over the edge, but damned if they won't find a way anyhow, some of them.

I started swimming back, and I have never been a good swimmer. In those days I was strong as hell and that didn't hurt my chances. But, as I flailed away, I was more and more aware of not getting anywhere, of the big slosh holding me suspended. I remember that I could see the shore and all the people on it, including my family. They were drinking beer, throwing the beach ball around and NOT looking at me. But all at once it seemed a long, long way to them, and not only were they unaware of my struggles, they couldn't have done anything even if I had been able to cry out. I was in a situation where either my will or skill (not much of the latter) coupled with a generous ocean, would preserve me - or I would drown.

I remember telling myself not to panic. I guess that is what the boy on the 62nd floor must have tried telling himself. Stay calm. Think. Use your strength in controlled waves and then in strategic bursts. If I had panicked and started wildly beating about, I would have died. At the time I didn't know to swim diagonally - which would have made it easier - but I just kept plugging away. I made it.

But I will always remember how far away everyone seemed. Not 100 yards away if you measured it, but they were in another country, living a different life. It's like when you know you have terminal cancer, I suppose, and you go to one of those parties where you used to have fun. They still welcome you, but they treat you, in a subtle way, like you are dead already.

(There is a funny side to this: the story of a man who is dying of something or other and conveys this information to the mailman - a guy who has been delivering the mail to his house for years and is almost more than just an acquaintance, indeed - like a friend. So the owner tells the mailman the sad news and of course the mailman is very upset and full of doleful commiseration and encouragement. This goes on and on. The friendship even seems to deepen because of the imminent tragedy. But eventually, after the expected date of death has been surpassed due to some improbable remission, and the guy's life goes on and on and on, the mailman starts to get pissed off with the whole deal. He starts to wonder, when in the fuck is this guy going to die? He feels cheated of his opportunity to grieve for the guy.)

But... I remember part of a poem that a woman wrote way back at the University of Florida in 1980–81, about the time Robin died, come to think of it. It was about a guy who committed suicide by swimming out to sea, too far to ever get back.
She wrote:

We want to know
how the blue lights looked
so far from shore,
such a long a way out
as the sea parted around you
like a spell.

When I was back on the shore that day, I could see that the Living had no idea that I had rejoined them from the Dead. Nor how close the two were...and are. At all times. People speak of yin and yang, and this concept is attractive to me, the idea that life is defined by the ultimate harmony provided by a marriage of opposites. The best authors, I mean the ones who are able to invent the most memorable characters, always do so by creating conflict. This is called making a 'dynamic' character where 'good' and 'evil', as it were, battle for control of the protagonist's soul, and they choose the human heart as their battleground.

But what I see instead is not any such balance at all, though I, too, strive for harmony and am gladdest when I find it. What I see again and again and again is the terrible fragility of life. How easily all the flowers you have planted can be trampled. I have this feeling when I see my dogs suddenly chase after a cat too near the road that runs through the village, and fast boys in fast cars might be surging through.

They would kill my dogs and keep on going. Or when my wife has one of her attacks of bronchitis, and her face gets too red. Or when my own heart skips a beat.

It can all end. Just like that. This is why, I sincerely believe, that watching a beautiful colt rush across a meadow, running for the sheer elation of extending its golden or jet black muscles and tendons without anything known as fear and with everything we call ecstatic celebration of life, sets my heart free. I am watching the horse trample death, beating it away with its proud hooves and down into the turf. And it doesn't matter that we all know Death will eat the horse alive in the end. It is that Fuck Death moment that I love. I watch the horse from my balcony, and I rejoice. Fuck Death.

Maybe the Chinese boy felt that way, too, but he didn't make it.

When I was out on the Atlantic Ocean that day, 50 years ago, I saw, as Yeats' wrote, "the murderous innocence of the sea." I was aware, like Icarus, the boys who flew too near the sun, of the supreme indifference of all that was around me: sky, water, people on the shore. In that sunny paradise, I experienced what I described earlier as "crumpling blackening vomiting nausea," as when Death looks you in the eye, and you know he's gotcha.

Something in me said, "Stay calm." I believe that Chinese boy heard the same voice: "Stay calm." I could have lost my grip. I could have gone under the lid of the sea as surely as he went down to be smacked senseless by an asphalt ocean of a different kind. Maybe that's why I kept watching that film. Because he was me, and I was him. Only for a few frenzied seconds. When I got back to the shore and staggered around trying to get my body and heart together again, I looked at the people, even my own family, and I felt: "You really don't understand at all, do you?" Well, how could I expect them to have?

Anyway, they are all dead now, and so I guess they understand better than I do.

It's what I think about these winter nights.

My wife builds a fire and then, after my day's work is completed, the dogs and I (they rest on the bed in my office while I give my eyes away to be eaten by the computer) go downstairs and sit on the sofa, one on either side of me. Often Thomas the cat leaps onto my shoulder. I ask Liuba to play piano and if she is not busy with dinner she does. And those melodies, once very simple but now gaining in complexity, provoke my mind to put away all duties and grievances and ambitions.

Tonight, I looked at my family and thought to myself, with indescribable happiness: This is it. I moved my eyes from one to the other of those magnificent, fragile living things, and I admonished myself: Love them now. Now.

For, in the words of the late Jane Kenyon (American poet), "*One day it will be otherwise.*" Yes. Otherwise.

That poor, misguided boy who fell such a long long way, I wish with all my heart that I could have been there and able to reach out with some wonderful great palm (which, alas, I do not have to offer) and spread it open, like a catcher in the rye, to secure and cradle him. And hoist him back up and plop him down on the building top and say, "Now go on, boy. And don't be so silly next time."

Olympian emotions - amid a feeling of dark shame for the cold-blooded thrill of watching him, not me, die.

DEATH IS NO LAUGHING MATTER,

EXCEPT SOMETIMES

It was in the winter of 1979 that I went to work at the Enfield Crematorium in north London. I was 30, divorced, and looking for a job. The ad in the newspaper said that a "chapel attendant" was needed. I called, thinking that some church official or secretary would answer, and that's when I found out that they were talking about a crematorium, I said okay. I understood the term, and that's about it.

So what they want, I told myself, is someone to put on a black suit and top-hat and pass out hankies to the mourners. One way to pass the bleak English winter and rake in a little dosh (make some money) as well. Anyway, I had always been good at pretending to be sad when I wasn't in the least, and faking happiness when I was looking for a rope.

It was a long bus ride, the dim-lit drizzle of afternoon narrowing toward dank, spittled evening when the bus stopped, and the driver nodded.

The bus churned away, leaving me at the gates of a large oblong building with a smokestack on top. Smoke was billowing out. In the field surrounding the edifice were many small cherry trees, mostly in their infancy and perhaps truncated by the cold - and before me was a sign that read "The Gardens of Remembrance."

I felt like the Land Surveyor in Kafka's novel *The Castle*. I was hired right away.

The next morning, I was ushered not to the chapel but to the fires below. I had two colleagues, Bill and Bob. (Really: Bill and Bob). Bill was the clever one, the "foreman", so to speak. That is, he planned out the schedule for the day. During the English winter a lot of elderly folks give up the ghost because of the "rising damp" in old ashen buildings. Their fragile lungs and hearts just cash out. And so Bill - and Bob and I - had a lot to do. Bill was a clean-shaven ex-WWII vet who had suffered shell shock at the front. So sometimes he still went crazy. Otherwise, he was fine - typical London working class wit - sharp and cutting - and he and his wife ran a DJ business on the side, catering to parties. The other guy was a fat comedian who looked a lot like Oliver Hardy from the classic old American comedy team known as Laurel and Hardy. Here was a geezer who had learned to take NOTHING seriously. Being in a crematorium actually fed his comic instincts.

For me, it started out different. During my life, I had tried to steer clear of dead people, and now they were going to start coming to me on a conveyor belt. Am I really able to do this, I wondered, as I put on my boiler suit that first day? It wasn't that I was particularly squeamish... the sight of blood never bothered me...it just sort of felt the same as it had the first time I held a live boa constrictor in my hands. "Am I really...?" Like that.

Let me explain the routine. There were six ovens, long and cylindrical, and sealed by easily manipulated metal doors on opposite sides. We would sit, bouncing balls against the walls, reading the papers, or just bullshitting, until the red light came on overhead. Then, like firemen, we would jump to our feet and run to the area where the coffins would be descending on a sort of dumbwaiter, as at a hotel when room service is arriving from the kitchen to the on-duty lackey who brings you your late-night order. We had a small gurney with us, and we would switch the coffin onto it while, up above, we could hear the melancholy organ piping out the appropriate strains, rather like Christmas carols for the deceased. Once on the gurney, the coffin would be dispatched to the designed oven. Bill or Bob would fling up the door and, like a rugby scrum, we would push it into the fire and slam the door back again. Then Bill and Bob, the senior members of the committee, would go sit down. My job was to expedite the burning process.

So, I would go around to the other side and open that door. The coffins being as frail as their customers, they succumbed rapidly, their wood vanishing in a trice while dropping their nails between the rollers which had let us roll the box inside in the first place. The bodies thus exposed, I noticed that they seemed to rise almost into a sitting position, like someone trying to get out of bed. I had the use of a very long spatula. If you have ever been to a pizza parlor where you can actually see the guy making the pizza, you will know what I mean. He opens the oven and throws in the doughy pizza, then periodically pokes and prods it until it is done. That's what I did. Except that the idea wasn't to cook the cadaver but rather to get the body to burn faster (we were so very busy that time of year), so that as it was whittled down by the fire, the bits and chunks of elbows, knee-caps, etc., could escape between the gaps in the rollers into the chamber below. The chest and head always took the longest to burn, And if the person had died of cancer, you could always smell the sweetness of the roasting, hissing tumors.

That done, the heap of white-hot rubble could be raked forward and deposited into a square metal box. I would take a gadget that looked like a pricing gun in a supermarket, but which was actually a magnet and pull out the unburnt coffin nails. We had a machine that looked like a large tumble dryer in a laundromat, and in would go these fiery, glistening bits and bobs. Within the machine were about a dozen very heavy iron balls - think of the Olympic shot put competition - and, once the machine was sealed and turned on, going round and round, the massive balls would grind the jagged pieces of bone down into a fine gray-brown powder. That would go into a small container with a label. Fred Jones. Lucy Brown. And off they would trot to the pantry storage room until further notice.

Except that sometimes Fred wouldn't fit. If he had been a large fellow, sometimes his remains produced more ashes than could be squeezed into the regulation container. So, even though the laws were strict and vehemently fixed in force, the unfortunate fact was that the part of Fred which wouldn't fit in his new plastic coffin went straight into the rubbish bin.

By late February, the rubbish bin was half-full and getting heavier by the day. Since I was the "new kid on the block" it befell me to carry the bin out among the fields and scatter the ashes - as a sign of compassion and to offset the fact that they had been in a garbage can. "Don't just sling them, scatter the bastards," Bill Lane instructed. "Show some f—ing respect!" I put on my raincoat - because it was pissing down -, donned my green wellies, and went forth. I scattered a bunch of those ashes, sure enough, but finally, I got tired and my hands were numb. I looked around and saw nobody was looking and flung the ashes out into the storm. A gust of wind chose that moment to assert itself and blew the ashes straight back in my face.

There was a pub nearby, and that evening after work I sat drinking and waiting for the bus. Every time I scratched my head a cloud of ashes flew out. People must have mistaken them for a bad case of dandruff.

On the long way home, I thought: this is what the guys at the concentration camps must have felt like after they had got over their initial shock at what they were doing and had become desensitized. It was just a job. You can get used to anything. I had gotten used to watching what used to be a man or a woman, someone's lover, change into a gasping, flaking, shrinking dot of flame, and then nothing but rough sand. What are you supposed to do???

Bill Lane had one streak of sentimentality in him. If it was a baby who had died, he would never let that infant enter the fires alone. He would wait until a dead woman came down and put them in together. The child in its little violin case, riding on the bigger box that held the Madonna. I liked Bill for that.

And every morning, part of my job was to go out among the grass and dig little holes for the ashes of the dead whose remains had not been claimed during the government-mandated waiting period of six months. If no one wanted them, if no one came with an urn to convey them back to a living room somewhere, then I, at the instruction of the fleshy, cold, gay Director in his starchy suit and reeking of pochuli, put them where they would be alone in death, as probably they had been alone in life.

And then my job was to plant a little cherry tree atop their ashes. That was why it was called The Gardens of Remembrance.

WINGS OF MY CITY

Much is made of how we say, in effect, "Hello." Think of all the books you can read about the ways to make a good "first impression." (The Americans always include a section on "selling" yourself.) Indeed, these methods of engineering a first contact have cultural implications. So Americans start out by being as friendly as a Labrador puppy, Brits at times like arch, aristocratic poodles, Russians like boisterous bears (well, of course!), etc. Be that as it may, what about how to say "Goodbye?" Surely, while a first impression is subject to change, a last impression is not. It is what we carry with us forever.

In Moscow, as in all huge cities, when the time for "До свидания" (*addio*, farewell, etc.) comes, you just might be disappointed if you are expecting a speech or farewell dinner. Often there is something in between a kind of glacial abruptness and a spy's disappearing act that lets you know that the party is over, your services no longer required. This happens not with casual, who-cares? acquaintances but with people who have been friendly. (I have begun to think that the word "friendship" needs to be redefined to factor in the nano-speed of modern life.)

This process of elimination is not confined to Russia, nor do all Russians employ the tactic in the Game of Goodbye. But it happens enough that I noticed, and I never noticed it anywhere else.

Yet it might be because the culture never has been predicated upon the durability of things such as infrastructure, businesses, or even city blocks. Unlike in America, where various check-and-balance institutions can keep the ship afloat until Congress finally agrees to sink only half of it, in Russia snap decisions are made by the Men in the Darkness, and what was there on Tuesday evening may be gone without a trace come Wednesday morning. The forces of the night will have swept it away.

I am not exaggerating. At least three times (when I worked in Moscow as an ESL tutor), I rode the metro to my location, hit the street and looked around only to be stopped in my tracks wondering, Where has everything gone? Had I left from the wrong end of the station? Was this the right stop (sometimes one is sleepy)??. The entire corner of a city block which the day before was full of lively sushi bars, pharmacies, crowded cafes, and small grocery shops was simply not there anymore. No warning. It eventually ceased to surprise me, just as it no longer amazed me when a crew would appear and tear up the street or entrance to a metro and then disappear, reappearing months later. No discernible logic. But what about the people who had worked there in the cafes and shops, the ones you saw every day and thought you knew? They vanished, too.

So, for me, it is about people. And these truncated endings have occurred in what I thought were reasonably well-established personal relationships. Let me give one example. A young lady I knew named Daria had long been a student and friend. We had even exchanged some intimate personal information over this several-year-long friendship. Then one day Daria disappeared from my constellation. Repeated messages and efforts to elicit a response having come to grief, I finally nailed her one day on Facebook. She said it was nothing personal, but that she had wanted to start her life over, and in order to do this she had to erase the past. And that was the end of Daria.

An extreme example, true. But not inconsistent with the general fabric of Russian mentality. What to make of this?

I had been in Moscow for a long time, and people would often ask for my impressions. I like to think of myself as mildly insightful, but I suppose I end up trotting out the usual cliches that anyone else might offer. A lot that is positive, a complaint or two, and other blah-blah on what has struck me as strange or remarkable. Nothing earth-shattering. I could talk about the *dacha*, the *remont*, the *babushka*, the Russian concept of how to celebrate a "birthday." But another time for all that.

I speak now only of goodbyes. Yes, life is full of them. In every hello there is an implicit goodbye; okay, that sounds a bit cheesy and contrived, like any second-rate pop song might express it. But it is true nonetheless, just as I believe that some lives are lived in the minor musical key, and some in the major. Some adagio, some presto. But in Moscow there is rarely much denouement, and God help you if you manage to offend someone. Best to have taken a photo along the way, because that is the last you will ever see of them. Complete obliteration.

Maybe there are too many explanations or attempts at explanation in this life. Sometimes it's best just to let it go. Or stay too busy doing stuff to get all muddled up with abstruse philosophical meanderings. But sometimes silence is very cruel when something should have been said in its place.

Imagine you have taken a lady you are in love with to a restaurant and at some point she says she's going to 'powder her nose.' And she never comes back. There you sit, nibbling on your pork chop or whatever, and at first you wonder (after 5 minutes) what in the hell is keeping her. Then you start to worry (after 10 minutes), even if you know very well that going to the toilet is usually not a cause for concern. Then you get angry (after 15 minutes - the waiter is looking at you funny). Then...after 20 minutes, a kind of desperation creeps in. As the days go by, you try and try to imagine what could have happened. Phone calls and messages do not avail. And you never find her again.

Sounds like a Murakami short story. Swallowed by air.

I have asked Russian people about this. Many think it's my imagination; others acknowledge it. Now don't get me wrong. I have a certain kind of personality that some people take to and some don't. Maybe I am too needy. Maybe I crave a lot of love and reassurance. Maybe I push too hard. As such, I have been told to Go to Hell more than once. Sometimes gently, sometimes firmly, sometimes vociferously. But that's precisely the point: in

America, they usually just say, "Go to hell." Or in England, "We are terribly sorry, but it is with great regret that we must hereby request that you please, if you don't mind of course, Go to Hell." Either way, it's okay because it provides a sense of closure. In Russia, they just expect that one day the truth, the cast iron reality of it all, will sink in. It has actually been explained to me this way. I am not kidding. The idea is that eventually you just say "Hmmmm... Well... I guess that's the end of *that*."

Look at it this way: coming from where I do (America), I have seen a lot of Hollywood films (but hasn't everybody?). Until I started living in Europe, I didn't notice this so much, but all American films, even the great ones, tend to preach a bit. They all have a central moral or message to deliver, and they wrap it up nicely at the end with a shiny ribbon. It says, "This is the point, get it? Do you get it? Well, do you??" It was instilled in me long ago to expect to be hammered by 'the moral of the story.' When I started watching European films, I had a shock. I would just be warming to some engrossing narrative when, all of a sudden, the credits would start rolling. "What the f---?" I would splutter. I hadn't even finished my popcorn.

But after a while I began to prefer the European style. For a start, the heroes and heroines – if they could be called that – were not always tortured emblems of physical perfection. They looked like real people. But it was the way the films ended, often stopping at a point that seemed pedestrian, almost empty of purpose-- like it should be a pause and not an ending -- that would trouble and perplex me afterwards. Strangely, the blase unfinished business of the film would torment more than any neat package or tidying up would have done. It was as if I were being invited to choose my own ending. Or was it just a different way of saying goodbye than I was used to?

Sometimes people return to my mind that I haven't thought about in a while. What brings them back I will never know. I wonder if I ever wander back to other people's memories in the same way? Do any of those people in the vanished shops ever think about me? ("Ah yes, that American guy who used to stop in. I wonder what he is doing. We never even told him 'see you around!'") It must be true, but somehow, I can't believe it. I think I am dead to them. So why do I think about them? Sometimes I just turn on lamps in corners of my mind, and there they are.

In some ways it is childish to pretend that something doesn't exist when it clearly does. I realize that I used to do it too, just blot out things from my mind that I didn't want to deal with. Like when I was a teenager and I would take my grandfather's car, promising to be back at a certain time. Instead I would get drunk and not go home. I would look at the clock and imagine him sitting there, seething and worrying, ready to kill me but secretly afraid that I might already be dead. I knew it. But I would just take another drink and forget about it.

It was the same in later years with wives and girlfriends. I would not call and explain why I was late. Once I did cocaine for three days and never went home. My young wife was very conscientious, and I would imagine her getting up, shaking off her despair and going to work. And I would drink more and do more cocaine and just pretend that it was a dream and that none of it really existed. But even in my haze, I would think of her and feel rotten. And then smudge it out and keep going.

And when I was a very young child having a tantrum after being scolded by my parents, I would hide my head under the pillow and make the world go away. In the darkness was denial. There was no world and therefore no responsibility.

Sometimes that is how the Russian goodbye makes me feel, only in reverse. That I am the one sitting at home waiting for some sort of reassuring voice offering a logical explanation. Instead there is silence. Now I am getting my own medicine back.

Of course, it is easier to do this in great cities. In a village you cannot hide from your cousins. I remember once seeing a middle-aged Asian woman riding the metro. She had two huge bags of groceries, but somehow on the way home she had gotten terribly drunk and had been sick. She was slumped over and the bags of food were sloshing about in a pool of vomit. Everyone glared at her with disgust. But at the next stop she miraculously pulled herself together and somehow lurched off the train. In an instant it was forgotten. In cities you can say goodbye to everything just by disappearing and you will be lucky if anyone cares. Or notices even.

In my search for reasons, I have been told that Russian people do not like to hurt your feelings, or that they are too proud to say that they don't have money for lessons, etc. Or that, in terms of taking English lessons, sometimes they become discouraged and just want to bury the experience, like leaving a suddenly unwanted pet dog by the side of the road. Just make it all go away. Ok, maybe so. But I mostly think it is more to do with Russian mentality, something I have to accept.

Older now, I champion the certain formalities, the certain rituals that most people, over the centuries, have thought it civil to observe. One of these concerns the taking of one's leave. That is, the proper way to say goodbye. In places such as America and England it is generally thought that one should do a bit of explaining. ("I am telling you to Go to Hell because...") And whether it is the truth or a half-truth or an outright lie, it is a handle you can grasp hold of. It is like calling leukemia - leukemia. It doesn't save you but it helps to call it something. This, or so the theory runs, makes it easier to accept your fate. On the other hand, an enigmatic refusal to engage, a shrugging of the shoulders when it would be better to come up with a few words that might put a frame around the rejection -- while this may appear poetic in books and films -- in reality it seems like a cold, heartless, even cowardly tactic. It is like abandonment. And one is left not knowing what he did wrong. Sometimes you don't even know at first that you have been told to Go to Hell. You think you are still in with a chance. You just have to wait until the Big Silence sinks in. Then you know. Go to Hell.

I guess it comes down to my insistence that things make sense.

But life isn't like that. The cosmos is a starry jungle, I believe, a wasteland of riotous swirls of molten heat, endless frozen tundra of blank space without oxygen, and black holes that any spy would envy. And more and more I think that this intergalactic jungle has no Boss.

So, when you die, when you drop dead on your way to the toilet and your lady is waiting at the table with her Caesar Salad, don't imagine you left anything undone - that's my advice. It was just another way of saying goodbye without saying goodbye.

One day she'll accept it.

BENEDETTA

End of the day, although what little there was of daylight lapsed at 4:00. Now, at 7:30 you leave the gray, Soviet-style building where you work and trudge among the boot-eating snow-porridge and ankle-ripping potholes, side-stepping and being side-stepped by one human shadow after the other. Everybody is in each other's way. It is the city's manner.

You used to be lonely at this hour, needing to get behind closed doors, back to your one-room apartment where you could pour yourself a drink and sit in your underwear, watching the inanities of the TV screen that threw babbling images your way. These phantoms mocked you, drearisome but seeming more alive than you. It was like one dead fish watching a sea of dead fish, you used to joke darkly to yourself.

Usually you went home by metro, but there were evenings you could not bring yourself to plunge into the packed claustrophobia of the frenzied trains. After a day of tepid office air and, at both ends, the raw smog of city asthma, the very idea of breathing human proximity, human trash, desperation, and anger, was beyond you. You were too angry yourself to face the anger of others.

So you walked. It wasn't that far - maybe thirty minutes on foot. Sometimes you had a quick beer in the alley to calm down.

Twice you had taken out a membership at the fitness center, but it never lasted. Aside from getting fit you had hoped to meet women. But it never worked. You were too shy or ugly, maybe your sweatpants didn't bulge out enough or your eyes were too hollow - whatever it was, the women you wanted never wanted you.

You had started to go crazy and have very sordid dreams. Sometimes in the great capitals of your sleep, there was mayhem. It was you, among the night devils, orchestrating mass murders, killing everyone as you grinned at them with your frothing, toothless gums, as in the films. Whole cities died beneath the cruelty of your countless weapons. But all that took place only among the nocturnal cobwebs. You would never do it of course. The citizens were safe.

You wanted love. But you couldn't find it. And it wasn't that it was just a step or missed bus or a heartbeat away, in which case, casino odds said you would get lucky. Even the fruit machines in gambling halls held out a kind of bizarre, addictive flatline which was marketed in terms of trampoline-like anticipation, kind of futile breathlessness somewhere between faked pornographic orgasm and genuine heart failure. But you had reached that stage where love was beginning to turn to hate. You studied yourself in the mirror - every piece of your face - and you couldn't detect anything so hideous. Nor were you an alcoholic or psychopath. So what was wrong?

What was wrong was that women didn't either like you or want you. And those few who liked you didn't want you. Again you checked the mirror. OK, a hive of minor blemishes - some treatable, others not, a jittery rebellion of trembling lips when you tried to speak of love and love's desires, teeth that were less than sharp ivory tusks from the elephant farm, yet...you were not repulsive. You looked like the photo of a worn-out soldier - slightly out of place and time - but not a beggar. Not shit. But you never had found a real lover. You drank the elixir of the cold winds and the fog of insubstantial weekends that were never restful, and, whatever else you did that was good, you confronted the increasing greyness of your life and played music well into the night, lost anthems of love and loss, and this was your way of showing them. But after you had finished showing them, then it was just you and the rain, and the innumerable sad mysteries the rain will tell you about but never help. All those spattering gusts ever did was confirm. It never perfected a thing except maybe to add roundness to ancient rocks So loneliness lit up your windows and also the windows of the city as perceived through your vision, although you knew, you just knew, that behind some of them all the methods and motions of primeval dances denied to you were swirling in rooms for reasons both obscure and tormentingly obvious.

It was because nobody wanted you. Why not? As a matter of fact, such unrequited love, however general and misdirected, was beginning to make you feel... well, alternatively suicidal and homicidal - now in daylight hours as well as in the middle of the night - as if you wanted to commit some great act of destruction. So you were seething with these gales of rage when you met her.

HER. You found her in a shop you happened to stray into along some anonymous alley. The shopkeeper introduced you because he apparently knew her well, and your mutual attraction was immediate. Indeed, you could not imagine ever finding this perfect woman in such a nondescript and dubious location. But there she was, looking brightly at you, answering you in a voice at once as open as the sea and as intimate as a tale told round a campfire.

You could tell that she wanted to be yours, She must have been some sort of foreigner, and maybe she didn't have documents, because it was necessary to pay the shopkeeper for his silences - and in fact, he demanded a rather great fee which meant a considerable drain on your bank card, but once that transaction had been carried out, it was simply a matter of taking her home.

In the metro, the women glanced at you with eyes batting out the usual avoidance, and some of the men, spying the kind of immaculate lady you had with you now, actually grinned, maybe out of a rich darkness where much masculine sexual fury lives, a surge of electric energy at seeing the essence of all things female rendered in this simultaneously sensuous and static form, and then each of them looked away as if they had been caught stealing cookies, and left the two of you to your own romance.

You asked her if she wanted to share a pizza with you, but she declined. However, she was only too happy to see you purchase a small bottle of vodka and a few cans of beer. She wanted you to be happy. Her eyes were exquisite, and her lips protruded, puckering in the way that seemed to request a kiss.

When you got her home, amazingly, she praised your forlorn little apartment, and her smile, out of nowhere, seemed to remove the whiplash of the years. Her voice, which at times seemed to come from a faraway machine, nevertheless understood the art of nuance and spoke to you in ways of irony, cajolery, and seduction.

She answered all your questions and waited patiently while you ate some pizza and had just enough to drink. She folded her hands while you showered. And then she allowed you to undress her, and when you entered her, doing so with a woman for the first time in years, and - because of your desperation - you finished in just a few seconds and lay there not knowing whether to cry out in response to the flash of ecstasy or from seething disappointment because you had spilled yourself prematurely - she told you in a caressing murmur that you were the best lover she had ever had. And said she was yours forever. Against great odds, you believed her.

In the morning you woke very early and watched her lying there with her eyes deeply closed. Your breath and armpits stank of the rancid flavors of sleep and you needed to relieve yourself. That done, plus a little freshening up of mouth and limb, and you returned to find her still the same.

Her body did not smell of sour flesh baked in blankets, but rather it retained the fragrance of the night before. She slept gracefully, more like a work of sculpture than a real person, but in this case, the immaculate hand of the artist had brought all desirable elements to bear. You wanted to say something to her, but for the first time, you felt a sense of apprehension.

What if she had changed her mind? Besides, what was there to say really? Was there anything that had to be said? Silently, almost holding your breath, you began to stroke her. Her eyes opened at once, gazing up at you like brightening emeralds that could speak all languages.

"Good morning dear" you intoned with your mouth to her ear as if to drive the words as deeply into her woven fixtures as you could. Passion was already igniting you, fostering a tingling craving. You felt bizarre, calling her 'dear.' Anyway, what was her name? Barbarella? Was that what the man at the shop had said, leering? You needed to call her something new, something to take the dollhouse marble with its hint of lifeless frigidity out of her eyes and replace it with a glow of the dawn sun rising over a harbor.

So, maybe Bridget? Chiara? Mona Lisa?

"Good morning, honey," she replied.

"Do you want me again?" you asked, more abruptly than you meant. You cursed the tremor you heard in your hesitant voice, the imploring sound of wheedling, of begging.

"Yes, of course."

Later…as you closed the door behind you to go to work you looked back at her again and called back, as if for good luck, "See you later, okay?"

"Goodbye, Honey. Have a nice day at work."

"Goodbye, Benedetta."

The name had jumped from your throat. It would be hers. It had a graceful and gentle quality to it, even something faintly religious…

It was only when you were once more immersed in the uncompromising rawness of the winter streets that you began to regain a certain...perspective. She isn't real, you know, you reminded yourself. She talks to you - about the weather, the Great Patriotic War, Spartak vs Dinamo, the Sanctions, the prices in the supermarkets. She talks about manicures and pedicures, and about trips to foreign countries. But this, all of it, is just made of the endless recording and computing of combinations of possible replies. She is a doll, and she doesn't care about anything. Why do you even call her a she?? And change her mind? Why, she has no mind to change!! How can she change what doesn't exist!! You even cringe a little bit when you imagine, not her but it - IT - filling one side of your bed in that grimy apartment, nothing more than an elaborate smorgasbord of technology, a labyrinth of plastics, silicon, and gel, all molded into the female form of the finest and most beguiling order. And you know, because you understand this wave of technology and all that it promises, that one day your newly acquired 'Benedetta' (as you have decided to name her) will seem as primitive as a Cro-Magnon woman.

But now it doesn't matter.

You ride the metro, somewhat surprised to notice that your reflection in the opposite window of the train appears more colorful and lively than the normal paste of that lusterless bulb of sagging tissue, the sort of death-in-life countenance your face had become. So you smile at a few of the ladies. They don't smile back. "Oh well, some things never change," you think, and yet today the sense of rejection and defeat is less. Becausebecausebecause... at your apartment, someone is waiting. Something - like a kind of caring Teddy Bear. Like several of those stuffed animals you had known as a child. But somehow more alive than any of this rabble and flotsam on the train.

Those Teddies, which gradually had fallen apart or been left behind like carcasses in the old buildings your family had carried you from... had been real in some lost way that now you knew remained valid. Like a bridge over scowling water connecting the animate with the inanimate, no less than prayers in the best places where real reverence is possible - if not in churches, then maybe in fields or valleys or even the cubicles of bus station toilets where the darkest meditations may come - connect life to death and vice versa. The apartment was not empty now. Something was there. And it would say hello to you at the close of day.

That evening, after having sex with Benedetta (and you noticed that this time you were more under control and could build the experience, even pausing in the middle to exchange tender words before continuing and climaxing), you spent a long while telling her your life story. There wasn't that much to explain, you had thought at first, but then you found yourself going on and on, as if trying to solve old vexing riddles. Initially, you were afraid that she would grow impatient and cut you off...but she didn't. She listened, agreed with some things, asked questions of others, and sometimes even challenged your opinions and conclusions. You were happy about this, glad that her designers had not made her a slave. That would have been boring, so much so that the illusion would have collapsed. And you had begun to grasp how important the illusion was.

You needed to be listened to, acknowledged, praised, accepted. Not exalted...well, maybe once in a while, as when she told you that you were the world's greatest lover, the best, the very best. But you could accept that it wasn't true. That no one had wanted you... Her artifice was trumping reality, and why should you care?

You loved being her hero. Her war hero, her businessman hero, her sex hero. Her best friend. Yes, that was important. Her best friend. That you were a man, not a cockroach.

The months passed, and little by little you began to understand some of Benedetta's limitations. There were ways, even as elaborately as she had been conceived, that left gaps, holes, patches of emptiness. For example, she could not fathom your occasional bouts of despair. If you got drunk, she did not admonish you. If you began to cry, she simply waited until your eyes were dry. If, in a poetic moment, you praised the sunset (as you both looked out on it), she would praise it, too. But you did not ever hear the passionate prayer in her voice that you heard in your own.

Yet, all in all, Benedetta struck a balance. She would argue with you but didn't defy you. She would complain of being tired and yet respond like a daisy under a spring shower to your touch. She was willing in the end to let you be the boss of your own days and to follow in that wake. As if you were the Boss.

But you didn't want to be the Boss. You wanted a companion. You wanted a friend that you could share your time with, who accepted you unconditionally and who did not grimace at your moments of failure. You wanted a friend who was always glad to see you. Benedetta agreed to be that. You are not the Boss, she said. You are my friend. Her eyes twinkled.

So you would make her comfortable in the mornings, sitting her in front of the TV and turning on what she had said were her favorite serials. At work, you thought about her, more and more and more, just as the other guys thought about their wives. You learned to deal with her limitations just as a devoted (if no longer panting) husband can deal with a wife that once beguiled him and now just occupies a place.

But Benedetta's limitations were not those of a human and therefore did not rankle. She had none of the crankiness, bitterness, and silent fury of a real wife. She was robust and sexual. She remained as young as a melon in the moonlight. You could not but notice that it was your hair, not hers, which eventually started to turn gray.

It was her birthday, a number of years after that first encounter, and you rushed home, bringing wine that only you would drink, and roses that only you would really see, no matter how much she thanked you. And you would make love to her again, screaming in the orgasm which only you would feel. And yet, somehow, strangely, you had become convinced that, even among those inner plastic folds and dials of hidden software, she would feel the orgasm too. A gradual awakening. As you became more like her, she had become more like you. She had begun to care too. You sensed it, and therefore believed it.

She sat in her favorite recliner evening after evening, making careful, often intimate conversation with you. During the first years, you had wanted sex every night, but gradually even that did not seem so important. You were just glad to see her, and you looked forward to the shows on TV also. When you were late, you apologized, and meant it. And you chose her birthday and other holiday surprises carefully. You brought home a kitten one evening, and she was delighted. You could see it clearly in her dancing eyes, even as the kitten watched her warily and in a different way than it looked at you.

You loved her devotedly, and would have walked, like a lamb to the slaughter, to save her from harm. Because she, your dearest Benedetta, had always been kind to you, and sat with you every evening when the sun was setting.

WHEN I WAS JUDAS

Twelve years ago I ended up in Germany. I seem to have a funny way of going on about where I 'end up'. For one thing it has usually turned out to be a temporary situation, so I don't even know if the term 'end up' should be applied. Sometimes fate (or 'destiny') - which in real terms has meant that I ran out of other options - has dumped me in a strange city or country, and then I have no choice but to repair to the nearest bar to sort out my next moves.

An old drinking buddy of mine once observed, with some acumen: "Eric, most drifters just go from town to town. You go from nation to nation. Anyway, I had recently spent a while in Italy, and it was from a small northern Piedmont city named Udine that I took off for Frankfurt-on-Main and then on to the Gothic town of Marburg, where I had been hired to teach English.

Actually, I was lucky to pick up the gig in Marburg because I sort of got stranded in Frankfurt with nowhere to go. You see, I had met this attractive German girl in Florence while she was on holiday there, and she invited me to Frankfurt. It took three years for me to accept her invitation because stuff kept getting in the way, and by the time I finally arrived either she had changed, or I had.

Or maybe it was just a case of seeing a woman (and I mean the female gender very specifically here) in her real life circumstances instead of the "help me unsnap this fucking bra, will you, Honey?" holiday mentality of numerous Snow Whites whose morals 'drift' into puddles around their stilettos when they think God and country are not watching. Could that have been the case?

In short, the fun-loving, devil-may-care, let's-experiment-with-our-wonderfully-creative-sexuality Teutonic Maiden Suzanne had transformed into the staid, stoical German Matron of whose gloomy temperament many quietly barbarous Brothers Grimm stories are constructed.

I had become skinny (formerly buff) and she had grown fat (formerly suggestively ample), and I discovered - always a death sign in a relationship with me - that she was now a savagely strict VEGETARIAN, to the point of claiming to suffer nausea at the mere smell of roasting meat, which must also have included the fragrance of my cock and balls because she showed no interest at all in those porky delicacies either.
Per favore, torna a Sorrento (or Firenze.)

That's the thing with vegetarians. It's not enough for them to silently munch their carrots and cabbage like any other good rabbit. No, they have to make value judgments.

Moreover, she revealed herself to have a bad case of the German obsession with ORDER which I had always heard about. A compulsion which, it must be stated, I lack in nonchalant abundance. Apparently - or so disgusted former visitors and live-ins have told me - my inability to see dirt where dirt is staring me in the face would bring tears to a tombstone.

I could never manage to put anything exactly where she demanded it go. Moreover, she would sort the garbage into about six different recycling bags (yes, the Germans really do this), and send me down to the bins with no-nonsense instructions to put them in the right place. At first I tried to follow orders, then I just started lobbing them in wherever my fucking mood directed me - symbolic of the shrinking path of our brief reunion.

Anyway, upon the winter night of our acrimonious parting, I spent a frosted Hell's worth of Yukon hours wandering around an area called Höchst on the coldest night of the coldest winter in German history since the Middle Ages. In short, she put me out and left me to freeze. Thank God rail stations exist because a night under a bridge would have iglooed my corpuscles.

But, like all things, that lunar ordeal drifted off into history, which brings me back to the reason I went to Germany in the first place: to understand German mentality. I wanted to know how the most talented people on earth this side of the Jews and Asians could have become the monsters that they became. I wanted to know if it was just *them* - some special thing about Germans, or if Hitler could have happened to anybody.

In fact, I found the Germans affable, even jovial on occasion, and very sensible and accommodating. When they drink a lot, an androgynous element seems to enter, bordering on the orgiastic. It's as though they deeply need both to control and then to shrug away the control and go wild. Now this can happen every Thursday night with rednecks in the Bayou of Louisiana, the difference being those swamp rats don't bother pretending to have any control over themselves whatsoever. The Germans pride themselves on it. And then have... gaps.

But, as I later discovered, there were *clues* of something darker, or maybe just strangely detached, that the mentality of Germans in general seemed to reveal. Nothing I could write a textbook about; however, I would say this: there appeared to be a *blind spot* in Germans - an absence of feeling/emotion where feeling/emotion should be... A word that could be applied here is 'empathy.' The Germans appeared to have an articulate, jovial, playful, affectionate...void...in their character.

For example, let me compare a job assessment situation. The Americans and the English make a sandwich out of it, tasty in the bread but a little shitty in the middle. First they say nice things about your work, then in the middle they tell you about your slip-ups and errors, and then they say nice, encouraging things again at the end - if they intend to keep you, that is. (Just don't let it happen again.) With the Germans, you may have done 9 out of 10 things right, but the whole interview will focus on the one place you screwed up. Not good for self-esteem, but the German idea is this: Why talk about what you did right when that's what we are paying you to do? Let's talk about what you did *wrong*, so we can help you.

I guess there is a 'strokes'-free logic to it. Almost admirable. The Germans want to see you get better, not pat you on the head for correctly reciting the alphabet. Efficiency. The question, I guess, becomes how much is your need to be validated and told that "Yes, the night is dark, but a beautiful sunrise will come" - or how ready you are to hear, "Yes, the night is dark, and morning will be darker if the Chief is disappointed in the miracle he expects from you."

So I ended up in Marburg, whose Gothic beauty - in der Altstadt, that is - remains intact only because in the latter stages of the Second World War the Allies, who were bombing the hell out of everywhere else nearby, didn't think the town, which in previous centuries had been the County Seat but had later gone out of fashion, important enough to obliterate.

I had been hired to teach English at a small school called Passmore College. It was run by an imposing woman - a fortress-like, middle-aged German national who spoke perfect English - and her sickly and in permanent decline Welsh husband who by now, I expect, must be languishing in a horizontal elevator that is stuck in the earth. The staff consisted of me and a Scottish guy named Andrew Kerrigan who eventually turned out to be a kind of long-distance friend.

Frau Passmore found me a small apartment, which was actually a loft atop a building owned by a rather devious and cunning German man who was married to a stylish Arab lady. (Arabs and Turks are not hard to find in modern Germany.) The ceiling slanted down so severely that you could only stand up as you entered the room. After that, it was necessary to crawl about on your hands and knees. On the positive side, the ceiling consisted of transparent glass through which one could look up at the stars. So in effect I had my own planetarium. I loved that, and on clear nights lying there gazing at the fiery constellations also allowed me to rest my broken back. Celestial.

For meals, a small kitchen was available, equipped with a stove and little refrigerator in which I - along with the several other tenants - could pack our food. There was a young Arab guy who attended university and was friendly. We used to chat a lot and there was nothing wrong with him, except that, like a lot of black guys on street corners in America, he had a bad habit of always fondling his dick while he stood by the table and conversed, often while I was eating. This did not sweeten the pot.

Right around the corner from the school was a fantastic fitness center complete with TV screens everywhere, racquetball and badminton courts, sauna and steam baths, a tremendous food bar with an extensive selection of delicious meals, and an area out back for people to sunbathe, which many did in the nude. I noticed that the Germans, unlike even the Italians (in a reverse order of what you might expect), had no qualms about group nudity. The only problem was that most of the ones who used this special area were older people, who sprawled across the lounge chairs like past-their-prime oxen.

But in the communal showers, it was not uncommon for a pretty female staff member to stride right through picking up wet towels without batting an eye while a lot guys were hosing themselves down, cocks flopping this way and that. Again, this struck me as being yet another example of the German ability to compartmentalize. In other words, the same girl might have been having regular sex with any one of those guys, but work was work, as sex is sex - two different things - and so a few dongs dangling in the shower was no reason for the girl to take her mind off the task at hand, which was to collect the discarded towels and not to ogle the swinging, soaking dicks.

Next door to the school was a snack bar called "Imbiss" (which in German means snack), and the food, mostly a lavish portion of French Fries and an impressive assortment of sausage, was more than plentiful. There was an exquisitely attractive little blond Albanian girl named Shyrete who worked there, and I got to be friends with her. She had a kind of sour, ill-tempered older boyfriend named Tomas who owned a Kniepe (pub) up the street and I used to go there to guzzle the suds and watch football.

Shyrete also had her own business which was a mobile massage operation. She would apparently drive to the location and administer the massage. Happy ending or not - I never knew, and I didn't ask. I thought about signing up for one of her massages, but (twisted logic, I know) I liked Shyrete so much that I didn't want to settle for paying her for a hand job, even if one was on the menu.

Looking back, I realize that asking her to massage and then masturbate me (if that was what the contract called for) was exactly what I should have done. It wouldn't have changed our relationship at all. In fact, it might have improved it. One thing I have learned about life is that turning your back on a sexual opportunity because of noble ideals is a mug's game. The prospective partner simply rolls her eyes, and the uncomprehending world is not impressed in the least. In my case, I am left with a tantalizing fantasy, but I would prefer the solid memory of a pulsating, throbbing, outpouring of love and lust into Shyrete's strumming and rapidly flexing hand.

Such scenarios are especially true in Eastern Europe. The girls there don't have time for American mind games and episodes concerned with unearthing some trauma from back when the odd prehistoric lizard might still turn up in your mental backyard, and the therapist calls for another year of meetings to identify the species. Nobody cares.

The school itself was up a flight of stairs in a multi-purpose building, and, much to the chagrin of the stout, cropped-headed Frau Passmore (who in general aspect rather favored Miss Trunchbull in Roald Dahl's *Matilda*,) I found myself spending more and more time there. Even on the weekends when there were no classes, I would go to the college and bury the day on the internet, interspersed with visits to the Imbiss (Shyrete) and the fitness center, where I soon started making friends.

"Go home! Let the college be the college!" Frau Passmore cried one day when, arriving unexpectedly, she saw a lot of my wet laundry drying on the backs of the chairs.

But 'home' was lonesome. I would walk along the narrow river where, at a certain stretch of milky green vegetation in the springtime, I could look at the rapids as they swam upon the rounded stones and take in the majestic old river-houses along the left bank. There was one particular place where *all* signs of modernity vanished (no electric wires overhead even, and long periods without aircraft grinding in the skies). I would just stand there and imagine myself in a long-ago century. Then I would go to the Old Town and climb among the cobbled streets to huddle at the foot of buildings born of the distant past. Beer and pigeons and passing people. And Gothic gargoyles. Serenity.

On Sunday mornings at the empty school, I began to notice that people were singing in one of the rooms next door, and afterwards those who had been singing would descend into the parking lot. I also picked up on the fact that a lot of them were speaking Russian. So I made it my business to find out why.

It turned out that they were the congregation of a church - a church for what was termed "Immigrant Germans." Broken down, what this meant was that a lot of them were Russians who had moved to Germany and were now trying to get used to the new culture. But this was no Russian Orthodox Church full of gilded, mysterious saints with long beards, but more like the Baptist churches you find in America, where people sing, the preacher gets up and delivers some kind of harangue, and then they pass the hat. If you are lucky, there is food afterwards.

Wheels turned in my head. You see, by this time I had reestablished contact with my Russian lady Liubov, whom I had met in Siberia earlier. But during the time I had to go back to America to tend to my dying mother, Liuba had given up on me and found a job in a pizzeria on a Greek Island. When I tracked her down via the agency which had first introduced us, and proposed marriage, she agreed to come to Germany. The problem was that she spoke English very poorly and no German at all. What the hell was she going to do in Germany?

The answer? A church full of Russians.

So, with thoughts and ideas clicking in my brain like the well-oiled clipper ship I have always imagined it to be - at least when the harbor is not full of fog - I decided that I must join this church and make friends with the Russians so that when Liuba arrived, she too could make friends with them.

The only problem was that I didn't believe in God and, without an ulterior motive, would no more have joined a church than enlisted in the army of a Third World country about to be bombed by a superpower.

So one Sunday I strolled down into the parking lot after they had finished, explained that I was an instructor at the English 'college' and asked (I can't remember whether in Russian or German), if they would mind if I attended a service the following Sunday. I was cordially invited.

The following Sunday afternoon (which was when the weekend service was held) I was there waiting when the first arrivals came to unlock the door. It transpired that the church was run by a man named Kornelius and his wife Nadia. I guess they were in their late 30's. He was an average-looking guy of medium stature who dressed in clean casual clothes, a wholesome community-linked fellow whose unremarkable appearance in no way betrayed his nut-hard intensity nor indicated the serious mission he had chosen for his life. Nadia was tall and good-looking and, as I was about to learn, possessed a wonderful singing voice. There were, I guess, 25 or so people who attended every Sunday.

The service was carried out in both German and Russian language and there was a screen where you could see the words to the songs when they were not in the book. There was a lot of singing and many church members took part. Kornelius would deliver a sermon - not shrieking and glaring and jamming righteous fingers into our eyes like the flaming pinchers of Hell - but just talking, addressing the people in German language. Usually there was someone there to translate his words into Russian. After the sermon and more singing, they would pass the hat around, and then it would be time to eat.

I never found out if this church was of a particular denomination, but, as I said, it reminded me a lot of the Baptist Church I attended periodically back in St. Augustine, Florida, except that *that* church grew and grew until it was almost an empire, whereas the one in Marburg was never more than a small, more or less family operation.

Several years ago I had started going to the Baptist Church in St. Augustine, Florida, not because it was Baptist but because it was the nearest one to my house. I figured that one church was about as good as another, and I started attending in hopes of turning my life around a bit after too much party time.

I remember how strange it seemed at first to encounter people on Sunday morning who did not look strung out or hungover, who actually appeared to have taken a bath and combed their hair - and for a while I bought into it. It didn't hurt that the pastor was a great storyteller who always used a currently unfolding national or world event, tied it to a Bible passage and connected the whole thing to something in his own personal life. He was very entertaining as he tried to save our souls, and, well, I always have been a sucker for a good story. Moreover, as it was a Baptist church, there was always a tremendous amount of food on hand. You could get fat in that church if you wanted. I doubt that I could ever *pray* my way into heaven, but had it been possible to *eat* my way in, I'd probably be there already, eternal bliss guaranteed and a great feast under my chin, wafting up its irresistible succulence.

The problem with religious people like this, indefatigable church-goers, I mean, is that as you get to know them the pink cloud gradually passes from above your head and you become aware of their subtle biases and animosities and pernicious peeves - the internal bickering that eats like a slow rot at the base of the church - the politics, and the business-oriented bullshitters who use the church as a smokescreen for making a buck.

It all comes out after a while and at this point you can interpret it according to your choice: (1) it's all hypocrisy; (2) it simply reflects the human condition, which - translated - means that human beings are basically beasts of the field in spite of their best efforts to pretend otherwise, and the bitter truth of human blood and brain is an apparently unquenchable appetite for self-aggrandizement, augmented - unlike their furry brethren of the forests and winged partners of the sky - by EGOs of seemingly insatiable cerebral gluttony.

That's the version I accept, the second one.

Among the congregation in Marburg were two English-speaking young women, maybe 27 or 28 years old - a blond named Victoria Koehn and a Ukrainian whose name was Nadia Romanenko. When you meet two such women, both young, both articulate, both beautiful - is it amazing and, I guess inexplicable, why one does not light a fire in you and the other one does.

In this case it was Nadia. She was tall, like a lot of women in that part of the world (Russia, Belarus, Ukraine, the Czech Republic, etc.), and dark haired. But it was her face - beautiful, angular yet full, with blazing, flashing eyes - like a bust from the ancient world - that stopped me in my tracks. Moreover, she was an absolute whiz at languages. She spoke Russian, Ukrainian,

English, German, and Italian. She could literally rattle them off. In fact, her German was so good that she attended Marburg University as a graduate student and worked a steady job in a food shop where she had to deal with everyday German customers.

The three of us became friends, but Nadia was the one I focused on. I was lucky because the church had Bible Study every night of the week and Nadia usually came. I started really liking her, but a relationship for real was out of the question. First, she knew I had Liuba (I was at least honest about *that)*, and second, her devotion to the Christian faith was so strong that sex was simply out of the question. I had the feeling that maybe she had had some erotic experiences before the religion kicked in, but that was always left to my imagination because she supplied only elusive details, and, besides, anyone can become a virgin whenever they choose, right?

But she was a complex girl with an unpredictable quality to her mind. When she had gone to visit her mother, who lived in Italy, the Italian guys had called her 'La donna con la testa non apposta" ("The woman with her head not in place" - or 'the woman with the strange mind" - to paraphrase). And so she was. They speak of the 'mysterious Russian soul." Ukrainians, I have discovered, have souls even more full of vanishing birds.

So I started attending the church every evening. In truth, I both looked forward to it and depended on it. It was a place to go, somewhere I felt welcome. I found myself liking these people more and more. I couldn't wait for Kornelius' Nadia to start singing on those otherwise bleak Sunday afternoons. You can speak of Laura Fabian, Barbra Streisand, Celine Dion, or whoever you like. On those Sunday afternoons, there only needed to be Nadia the Preacher's Wife.

'Nadia' is short for надежда - pronounced Na-dyehz'-da. It means 'Hope'. Like вера ('Vera') means Faith, and Любовь means 'Love'. In English, these common names that to me always have sounded magical in Russian language, hit the floor like a sack of bricks. 'Hope Boone.' 'Faith McGillicuddy'. 'Love Snodgrass.' Doesn't work for me.

In church I used to feel like a hypocrite because I felt I had to pretend to accept their teachings. What was I going to do, argue with them? Dispute them? They had become my family. They prayed for me. They fed me. They acted glad to see me. And I wanted to be there. But it was the companionship, the non-judgmental acceptance and encouragement that I both craved and appreciated. Not *God*...Or was it maybe God in a different form? I still can't say for sure.

Yes, I grew to love big, tall, eccentric, ravenously beautiful Nadia. I drove the Passmore's van to out-of-town lessons, of which there were a fair number, even though I had no drivers' license - (I had said I had one, otherwise no job) - and when they were away on holiday, I used to cruise out and get Nadia Romanenko, who lived beyond the town, and take her home in the evenings. When I drove her to where she was residing, we would kind of hide because she didn't want the church people to know that we were seeing each other like that, and sometimes we went for a last walk in the fields before she disappeared inside. She often took off her shoes to tramp barefoot in the grass. I loved the beauty of her long, shapely, immaculate feet, which were like those of an ancient goddess.

And when there was no van to drive, I would walk with her after Bible Study to the train station, and we would sit in a corner of the station's cafe while we waited. It would be night then, and we would find a table. I'd grab a beer and she would have tea or juice, and we used to talk for a while. I never wanted those minutes to end. She would open up to me then, and from those fleeting opportunities I learned (and what I didn't learn, I sensed) about the travails of her earlier life. Maybe she cried once or twice, without ever saying why. Then I would go to the edge of the tracks with her and hug her before she got on board. Hugging her was better than sex, or maybe it just had to seem that way because it was all there ever would be between us. Watching her get on the train those dark German evenings was like…*Casablanca*. And afterwards I would walk home, maybe 40 minutes, just thinking about her, maybe stopping for a doner kebab if the place was still open.

I spent a lot of time at the university with Nadia, helping her to finish her doctoral thesis in English. It was a study of the difficulties which immigrant Germans (Russians) have in adapting to the new culture and different language/work/social demands. I learned a lot about Noam Chomsky during that period. I would sit in the library all day at Marburg University and put her work into the King's English. It was, as I remember, a great pleasure. She would come in the evening.
If she was using me, I didn't care. Even without sex, I was devoted to her, Nadia had a slight skin problem which marred her appearance ever so slightly. Other than that, she was a tall, superb Ukrainian girl with a wanderlust spirit buried within her devotion to the Christian faith.

One day in the summer, Victoria and Nadia and I went to a public swimming pool, and I saw Nadia as close to naked as I ever would: her peerless, sculptured face, her strong amazon body in a modest and not at all revealing dark bathing suit, her long coltish legs, and proud, summer-reddening, iron ore toes. Sighing, I drank her body into my soul. Nadia Romanenko. Well, she was just one of those girls that, like all of us, are the simultaneous creations of hymning Heaven and groaning Hell. One of those people you know and never know at the same time…but never quite forget, which is where the balance ends.

But the time came for me to leave. The good Frau Passmore and I had fallen out and she had secretly hired a new teacher. She and her husband told me I was fired at what was supposed to be a teachers' meeting to prepare for autumn classes. Any way you cut it, it was a shitty way to treat someone. But I had seen it coming, and already had told Liuba not to worry about Germany because I had decided to return to Moscow. Good move, because in Mother Russia my life just got better and better.

The people at the church bought me a brand new suitcase and Nadia the singing wife of Cornelius gave me a CD of the church songs because she knew how much I loved them. They went out of their way.

"My Cup Runneth Over" - those words from Psalm 23 in the Old Testament came into my mind. Kornelius gave me addresses to churches that I might find in Moscow. I forgot to look them up.
It seemed they never thought to ask themselves if maybe I was an Unbeliever and had been one all along. That I was silently laughing at them when I attended a special evening as they combined forces with another church and 'spoke in tongues' - before the Big Meal of course, which was what I was waiting for - chuckling inside at the foolishness of it all.

Speaking in tongues means a lot of unstructured - to me crazy - jabbering in a 'language' which in fact is designed to wipe language away, a kind of bizarre beehive buzzing which presumably God understands although other humans cannot. Nor could birds in the trees nor wolves in the forest follow the course of such racket at all.

Listening to it, that ranting mumbo-jumbo, that idiot's miracle of nonsense noise - I sat silently mocking them, asking myself, "Have They Lost Their Minds??" Did they know who I really was in these moments of their rapture? Did they know - or care - that I thought them fools? Apparently not.

But they were not fools.

I came into their midst as a stranger. I have always been a stranger. I am sure they saw this and made allowances for it. They were kind and gentle. They were good people. Of course, within the church there were disagreements. Even Nadia

Romanenko had trouble with her Christian roommate and finally moved out. Well, it's the human way.

So I went back to Russia, which was where I really belonged. Liuba came to me in Moscow and we got married and have been together ever since. After a few rough patches along the way, we have found happiness. We are mostly peaceful with what life has offered and what we have built with those offerings.

Nadia eventually - so I heard from Victoria - married a German man that I assume appeared out of the church. All that happened after I was several years down the road, and I don't know any of the circumstances. I will never know. Victoria sent me a photo of them, and he looked like a regular German guy, whatever that is. Impossible to know if good or bad. Nadia must have decided that he was the one. Then Victoria too disappeared, so no more snatches of information came my way. That was that.

By now I have mostly forgotten Nadia; anyway, she eventually changed into whoever she is now. Don't cry for the sparrow; it doesn't cry for you. But remember the morning tweeting of the ephemeral.

I remember so well those many evenings of Church and Bible Study. I tried, I tried, and I tried, but in the end I never believed a word of it. But I somehow believed *them.*

Their goodbyes and good wishes - and that new suitcase - born of a Christian spirit which they exemplified, live in my heart today as I write this.

I didn't believe in their God. At least, O at least, not the way they would have wished. Not the way I myself would have wished. Not that way at all. But as I listened to their songs and words, sat at their table, ate their food, and spent my hours with them those winter, spring, and summer evenings in 2008, I grew cleaner.

They were bathing me. Washing me all along with accomplished movements of gentle towels that gloved warm hands. Fanning me dry. Anointing my head with oil, you might even say.

I didn't know it then, but though I remain the same fool I always was in many ways, in some ways I hope I have grown wiser. They had Judas in their midst, but that didn't stop them from feeding this Judas and buying him a nice new suitcase to send him on his way to the future he said he wanted. Probably they knew me from the start.

As Christians, they knew they had signed up to love their fellow human being. But it was personal too, never doctrinaire. Never, you must do THIS. You must do THAT.

They accepted me and fed me. And sang to me.

And spoke in tongues.

THE NARROW ROAD TO THE FAR NORTH

I was having a spirited conversation today, early, with a really bright man - he was frying breakfast eggs while talking with me on Skype (the ONLY way to eat breakfast !) - about the best way to go about living one's life.

Of course, the thing about this very bright man (aged 47 and me -- a stout 69 as of today, 8 May) is that both of us have turned out more or less successful despite all the stupid things we have done. Successful in different ways, I should really emphasize.

He is a businessman. He has been both a very high-flier indeed, and occasionally (O how the bitter truth slips out once in a while'), a "low flier" too. But he has, seemingly, the wonderful ability never to panic. (Why do I always feel the need to qualify everything with 'seemingly' or 'apparently'?)

Always smiling. Some people smile too much, and my friend gets close to that edge, but nightmare never rules him. If it ever has or does, he is either The Second Coming of Harry Houdini (slipping the handcuffs) or the best-performing liar who ever lived. And I sense he is neither. Just a good guy who could smile his way through a heart attack.

That's him. Cheerful.

I am an artist, a writer, a teacher. In Moscow I can say (maybe I flatter myself) that I eventually became a small man's entrepreneur/businessman. A pretty-much-former drinker and doper (the beer stays, the rest has disappeared) who finally got it right and started to maximize. Avoided ass-plopping to a seat in front of the metro station among the Homeless or settling for a lying down spot in the graveyard in Snuff City...by no more than a hair on my chin. I should have been dead by now.

I have had five wives, my friend has had two. He has five children, I have two (that I know of). And so, to cut to the chase, we were talking about the best way to get the most out of our lives, And so my friend, whom I will call Boris, started telling me about his plan to start giving life-lessons to people in order to help them get in touch with the (business) angel inside of them. And charging them a helluva fee to do it (well he IS a businessman). Maybe you get the drift? Motivational stuff. Speeches. Books. There are many motivational speakers in America and the UK, for example, and some of them "earn" more money than doctors, lawyers, pop stars, and footballers.

I wasn't convinced. The difference seemed to come down to this: Boris told me that, as far as he was concerned, I had only "actualized" 30% of my potential. (I am, I repeat, 69, so this bad news was about as welcome as a root canal minus an aesthetic.) As soon as he said it, I knew he was right, but - squirming in my chair - I harrumphed a bit, and said something inconsequential like ""Not necessarily, my good man! And what about you?"

More bacon, more eggs. More coffee. "15%".
Okay. Not good news for either of us. But something of a relief to me. What to do?

Well that's a question that my friend Boris usually has an answer for. And he did this time. He told me about a chap named Tony Robbins, and this proved to be good advice and a good introduction. Tony Robbins sits at the top of the heap of the motivational world. I checked him out, and I can vouch for him. He's damned good.

But then Boris asked me a pointed question based on the 30% estimation. "What could you have achieved," he proffered fiercely, "if someone had told you or taught you how to maximize your potential prior to your doing all this COLOSSAL FUCKING UP that you did??? Huh?? You could have been the owner of a publishing house, or at the very least the Head of some English Department at some college or university. Or you

COULD have been a Pulitzer Prize winner? Yes???" Yes. Maybe so. And what, Boris, what could YOU have been?

A moment of brotherly love passed between us. Boris, not being a charlatan, Philistine, or otherwise shallow person, had the right idea: it's about life-features as well as money. But (he IS a businessman) MONEY was at the end of it. Money is the Fox that calls him and his inner Hounds into the depths of his inner Forest.

Boris turned the eggs, repositioned the bacon, hotted up the coffee, and said simply, hushed as a priest in a great cathedral: "More than I am now."

Pause. Then he resumed. His message was, IF you had had the right advice (motivational speaker), you would have identified your goals and become the Head of/President of/CEO of... (you fill in the blanks).

My message was, I have listened to many Motivational Speakers: my dad (the absolute best); taxi drivers, bartenders, whores, nuns, college professors, judges and jailors, wanderers and pilgrims, seekers, optimists, pessimists, evangelists, nihilists, communists, capitalists - and in the end, I always did what the hell I knew I was going to do in the first place.

In short: the great advice I heard in the past helps me write blogs NOW; it did not help me to live better THEN.

So, Boris and I agree that motivational advice will help.

We disagree on WHEN.

Boris thinks that by prioritizing upon receiving good instruction, you can find your way to the mountain peak under the North Star in a short time. That's because Boris thinks there is a Magic Pill.

I say that the North Star is much further away than it looks, and if you take the narrow road to the far north (I was once beguiled by thin Asian book bearing that name, and though I never read the book I remain attracted by the haunting suggestiveness of the title) you will meet many apparent dead-ends and need to take countless detours along the way, and on the sometimes rough and scraggly path you will feel certain you are losing valuable time. OK, for sure - but you LEARN.

Maybe one form of learning makes the businessman. The other form makes the poet.

Like that wonderful book *Stuart Little* (you know, the one about the mouse who is adopted by a human family and which is only partially a "children's book"), I choose to travel north in hopes of finding the little bird that I love. And like the end of that book, I try, guided by a compass in my soul, and with a Zen-like optimism, to find what may never be.

Maybe my bird is not there, maybe my beloved is long dead under whatever crushing fate. But I travel that road nonetheless.

Boris travels the main thoroughfare, yet always looking for shortcuts, ways to avoid the congestion, the human forest blocking his progress. And it is because he wants to pierce this congestion that he nevertheless immerses himself in that he must discover some measurable, countable means of profiting from it, ways that will render such a life meaningful to him. He wants the reward, the beans piled up on the table, and he deserves it because he is essentially a nice and good man. But my reward and his reward are different. He is looking for a golden bird, an imperishable emblem. The bird I am looking for may have died along the way, headed south, or found other friends.

What he thinks has been a waste of time - something that could have been avoided - I see as part of the pilgrimage necessary to find the little winged and blessed friend who flew away that day.

I heard a guy in an English pub say long ago: "Life is a Shit Sandwich. The more bread you got, the less shit you have to eat."

Boris wants a way around eating shit. He thinks, I believe, that if he can climb to the highest office with the highest windows, the shit will evaporate. Or, if not, HE, Boris, will be the one dispensing it. He wants to motivate others to think the same way. Wisdom for a Fee.

He says that the money they must give him is a very small investment for what they will receive in return...and, anyway, their money signals COMMITMENT.

Boris is right of course, in his way. The keys to the kingdom always come at a price. Even God knows this, which is why the Church asks us for our money.

I may read a self-help, self-motivating book or two along the journey, why not?

But I believe that the true way - my true way - is long and there are few if any shortcuts. Probably none. It is the narrow road to the far north that I am on, seeking a little bird that I hope to find waiting for me aloft on some sweetening branch of a cherry tree when the snow is falling.

I have asked people along the path if they have seen my little bird and they shake their heads.

No...

No.

No.

So, I turn up my collar and keep walking.

FORGIVENESS SUNDAY

Although I am in Bulgaria now, I was reminded yesterday of something I always thought was beautiful in Russia - the part of Maslenitsa, the Sunday of that week, when people are supposed to ask forgiveness from those they feel they have wronged. They also prepare 'bliny' - which are thin crepe-like pancakes that can be doused in jam, smetana (sour cream) vanilla sauce or whatever you choose. When I would go from one place to another giving English lessons in Moscow on that day, everyone would stuff me with delicious bliny. By day's end, I would be waddling along toward the metro station, absolutely *full*.

But I am not sure about the 'forgiveness' part. It is a great idea, and to me, though I am not much on religion, being able to forgive an enemy, or - which is even more difficult - a friend, would mean reaching the summit of a spiritual Mount Everest. Not everyone can do it, and I'm not sure I can. I think I like the *conception* of forgiving someone whom I have decided needs forgiving - the sort of "friend comes enemy becomes friend again" sequence - but for me would require being touched by what amounts to celestial amnesia, if not a paradisiacal form of Alzheimer's. But, as I said, I like the idea.

One the other hand, perhaps it is you/me who needs forgiven, and here it crosses my mind that there could be a degree of opportunism attached. I mean, suppose pissing off your business partner had cost you beaucoup big bucks, and a hearty "I'm sorry, mate/buddy, let's get back on track!" might put you once more in the hunt? Or supplication on bended knees before your estranged lover might land you back in the sack? In those instances, only a fool would fail to capitulate.

But let's pretend that the interaction is based on sincere impulse, maybe even after a long period of excruciating remorse. Additionally, let's pose the question: what does it mean to forgive someone? And why, if our hearts are in the right place and our intentions honorable, should either we or they need to come groveling for a pardon in the first place?

There was a famous film many years ago which was called *Love Story*. It was about two Harvard kids who fell in love. Unfortunately, the girl contracted leukemia and in those days it was a sure death sentence. So the film was a tear-jerker, and the most provocative line that came out of it was when one of them - the dying girl, I think - said, "Love means never having to say you're sorry." Her words went, in effect, viral (back when nobody thought to say "It went viral"), and a lot of people debated how true her statement was. I interpreted it to mean that if you really love somebody you don't go around doing bad things to them that you later need to apologize and ask forgiveness for. And in the best of all possible worlds, you wouldn't, would you? But of course, there is another saying: "You always hurt the one you love" - and I think that one gets closer to the mark in the real human junkyard we live in.

It seems to me that when two people fall in love, they begin with the great fiction that they adore each other so much and understand each other so well that they will never fall out nor experience a single emotion of dissonance or dissent. But naturally they do. I don't mean a harmless little spat; I mean that something will happen which causes one or the other to really lose it. During the shouting match that ensues, Romeo and Juliet see, in full force, just how ugly and hateful the other can be. Afterwards - at least while the relationship is still fresh - they kiss and make up and break the bed down with their renewed passion: thunderous groans and ear-splitting shrieks of unbridled bliss. Just to show they are really sorry.

Nevertheless, a poisoned seed has been planted, and I can attest to the fact that, after that first volcanic eruption, things are never quite the same. You have seen the monster in the other person. Moreover, what normally goes down is that, as the shine inevitably fades from the two golden apples - and contentment is replaced by bouts of peevishness and whole winters and

summers of slowly metastasizing boredom -- the pair begin finding faults in each other, and in many cases start acting like lawyers: meticulously compiling a dossier to tabulate, like a taxi meter adding more to the fare with each click, the misdemeanors and felonies of the other person. In the end, it is not uncommon that they start literally hating each other. Funny that, isn't it - how often you end up hating the very one you set out to love?
It's sad.

After the break-up, divorce or whatever, a l-o-n-g cooling off period is needed before the two parties can begin to think rationally again. In the event they have had children together it is often even worse. In the final stage of this melancholy farce, most often when they are so old that they probably wouldn't even recognize each other if they crossed in the street, some of them 'forgive' the past (some don't) Now, to me, that's REALLY sad. Why? Because by then it doesn't matter anymore. The time to forgive meaningfully evaporated long ago. Religious people would argue with me on that, but my reply would be "What's the point of saying hello when it is time to say goodbye?"

There is another issue here. Forgiveness is often coupled with an additional word, and it comes out in a binomial: "Forgive and Forget." The problem is that true forgiveness cannot happen without the second idea ('forget') coming into force. Many times, I have heard people say, "I can forgive him/her, but I will never forget." But how is it possible to really forgive someone if you feel you must remain forever on your guard, if, in the back of your mind, you remember (bitterly, for how can it be otherwise?) the nature of the offense?

So maybe we never forgive; maybe we merely agree to 'excuse'. There is a Russian saying that a friend quoted to me recently. In English it comes out something like this: "Russians don't love '*because of…*', they love '*in spite of…*' I can interpret this in two different ways. (1) We have to love SOMETHING, and imperfection is all we can ever expect; and (2) - which I prefer - we should try to love the whole person and accept this person as he/she is, without adding up the score of pros and cons: (Pros 7, Cons 6 = OK, it's a split decision, but it looks like love wins out.) No, the second option suggests that we embrace the whole, the sour with the sweet.

Strangely, it seems to be those with the highest principles of right and wrong, not to say the highest intellect, who find it hardest to forgive. They are the idealists who, once violated, never deign to stoop again. But to me, this is rather like the person (usually a woman) who, disappointed (or dumped) in love the first time, refuses ever to open her heart a second time. Better - to my mind - the brave ones who 'take a lickin'' and keep on tickin'' (no sexism intended here because it works both ways). In short, those who keep coming back for more.

Conversely, it's the more sleazy, shady folk who seem able to forgive without much of a problem. Or is it simply because, being cynical about both themselves and others, they have lower expectations from the outset? I mean, how can you be surprised if a prostitute or a crack addict lets you down? Alliances in a den of thieves come and go, and no one is astonished if the guy who helped you rob the liquor store last night absconds with your share of the take the next day.

I hated quite a few of my classmates when I was between the ages of 13-18. I was never a pushover and no one ever stole my lunch money, but somehow I never seemed to quite fit in, and back then I wanted to. I wasn't one of the 'popular' kids, which is so important to the cliquish Americans. I felt left out, even laughed at, and I despised the ones who seemed so cozy and comfortable inside their group and, above all, inside their own skin. I could never figure out what I was doing wrong. It's like the guy who breaks down and asks: "What am I doing wrong???" And they stare at him for a moment and say either "If you don't know, we sure aren't going to tell you" or (my favorite): "We don't know, but you just did it again."

I have a friend from back then who is something of a genealogist and who still goes to the high school reunions. He turned out to be the key that unlocked my past. Gene has sent me many photos of students from the Class of 1967 (I therefore know which of them are dead), and I see them as they are now - a far cry from back then, as you might imagine.

Most of them look like hell. The lady-killers and tough guys of that bygone era now make up the gray and faceless ranks of the elderly, most of them; they just look harmless, they who were capable of causing so much harm. Those much sought after girls... oh well... and those cool, savage guys... oh well.

I hated them because I felt they rejected me, because, for a while, I wanted to be like them, and I was never invited to the party. When I looked at some of those photos, I remembered: angry anecdotes rose from the graveyards of half a century ago, and the animosity still seethed in me. I enjoyed gazing at their ruin and imagined myself showing up at a high school reunion and beating the shit out of them (forgetting that I was now the same age and looked just like them). But do they remember me with such malice? Do they remember me at all? Am I refusing to forgive something, mostly imaginary, on which the statute of limitations expired ages ago?

I am reminded of a cowboy series that used to be on American TV. In one episode there was a guy who had had his right arm shot off by some villain long ago, and for the next 50 years he practiced shooting with his left hand, perfected it, and plotted his revenge. Somehow he got wind of the fact that his old nemesis would be arriving by stagecoach at a certain town. So he went there and waited, figuring to settle the score at last.

Still blistered by hatred, he watched as the stagecoach arrived and the people got out. But he didn't see the guy. So he shouted out, "Was Bill Johnson on this coach???"

And one little old fellow with a bad limp replied, his voice weary and bewildered, "I'm Bill Johnson. Why? What do you want?"

Television used to be good, and there were many great script writers. This was one example. The man with revenge in his heart looked stunned. He was expecting to see Bill Johnson as he had been half a century ago. So he glared at the old gaffer and cried, "Don't you remember what you did to me back in '77?"

The old man looked even more perplexed and he just stared for a moment at his would-be adversary.

Finally, he said, "No, I have no idea what I might have done to you. But whatever it was... I'm sorry."

I'm sorry.

And it was said with a profound sincerity even though the old fellow had no idea what he was supposed to be sorry for.

Then he kind of sadly shook his head and limped away, leaving the other man choking on tears of rage, frustration, and, above all, a kind of grief that neither words nor 50 years of vindictive fury could ever hope to express.

A couple years ago, Gene sent me a video which was a collection of photographs, one after the other, accompanied by a country music song, the saddest fucking song I ever heard. And the photographs were all of students from the Class of 1967 at Stonewall Jackson High School in Charleston, West Virginia, who had died. I remembered most of them, and in fact there were three girls: Francine Huffman, DeeGee Beckner, and Nancy Holbrook that I had, as they used to say back then, 'necked with'. An old friend, Harold Cavender, who died at age 17 or 18 in a motorcycle accident and whom I wrote about in a different essay, was there, too. For a minute, it was like lunch time again in the cafeteria at Stonewall.

There was no one among that black and white clip of photos (which seemed to go on and on) whom I had really despised, although, as I have said, those years were not happy ones. But seeing them all dead like that, well, it worked a number on me. Naturally, it reminded me that I am headed that way too (just a matter of time), but it made me understand that for all they ever said or did, whatever they themselves loved or hated, they were finally just transient, ephemeral little beings long since crushed under the weight of the universe. They weren't there to fight me. There was no fight left in them.

And so it meant that if I still had any resentments or arguments to make, I'd have to make them to myself. They were untouchable now. I could do all the forgiving I wanted, if it seemed necessary, and none of them would hear a word I said, not even the sound of me crying.

THOUGHTS THAT DOMINATE

I started thinking about all the faces I had seen during my ten years in Moscow. Maybe a million or maybe two. Or twenty. And I wondered, suppose I could make a photo album of them, selecting who I wanted. Who would I choose? The mainstays, the major players - or a bunch of images darting here, darting there?

Some of both. The people known, the women coupled with or called to, the men of friendship, of course they would stand at the front door of the gallery or museum, greeting me like the true hosts they always were. But further back in the museum would be the ghosts, the phantoms, a view (at last!) of the faces of female choruses on the midnight radio, the fleeting glimpses of nameless seducers leaving the trains, and the zillion glances across the abyss of street and air of which Human Time is constituted.

I guess they (the ones lost) mean the most to me. I say it like this: real friends make real deals. Their deaths bring real grief. And real memories. But the ghosts we met along the way, they signal something elusive and unattainable: the balcony, the vineyard, the village green, the totalitarian buildings from which young women emerge with winking poetry hidden like spies in their grey-blue eyes...

Always, endless and tantalizing. So - and I know it - in some such realm I would have cocktails with my greatest friends, and then I would slip away, slip away, slip away, to other places.

I was born that way.

As my ordinary date with perfunctory death nears like a train three stops away, I see the funny side of things. Maybe the ironic and the absurd also. I smile about what goes against the grain, defying expectations. For example, I remember one early morning on the metro in Moscow when two young policewomen got on together and sat down. One was a pretty blonde, the other brunette and not bad herself. They were in full uniform, but there was no wall signifying baleful authority separating them from the other passengers. They sat together and shared an iPod. Eyes closed, they listened to the music happily. Imagine something like that in America, and you can't. I would have taken a photo with my little black, outmoded hockey puck of a phone, but it didn't seem right to do that, so I didn't.

They were, in those early morning moments, beyond their uniforms and badges. They were pagan girls with laughter in their faces and their minds. And so the police uniforms were not an alienating factor but rather a connecting one: the presumably inevitable division between police and non-police dissolved. Just girls. Then they remembered, smiled, brushed off their uniforms, got off at their stop, and went to work.

I remember two guys with missing fingers. One had a kiosk back in the old kiosk days before the next jackass mayor closed them all down, That was in Выкино, and the 'finger-challenged' guy sold, among other things, chicken roasting on a rotisserie spit. Everybody said, don't buy chicken on the street like that, but I did, and it never hurt me. In fact, it was better than what you would find in a restaurant. I didn't speak Russian, and he sure as hell didn't speak English, but somehow, we both knew some Italian. And so, we became friendly. He was the first Russian face that said Welcome to Russia. Heavy-set, chubby, in all respects, nondescript and forgettable, that was him...except I didn't forget him. Never will... There was something... transparent... about him that can't be taught or faked.

The other fingerless man was a big, lumbering guy around my neighborhood who I found sleeping on the landing outside my apartment with some alcohol-sodden hag who would have made a great client for Jack the Ripper. My wife screamed at them so much that they finally woke up, but I slipped them some money, and ever after that this guy treated me as a fellow tramp, albeit a 'rich' one. He looked at me like the dog behind the fence you have given treats to. The dog is waiting. The dog is expectant. But he loves you in his way because there is nothing else to love. And no one else who cares. The dogs know that, and so did this man... I gave him handouts when I could not avoid him (which I tried to do at times when I saw him from a distance and wasn't in the mood to pitch him any freebies), but when I ran into him I treated him like any other friend or acquaintance. I didn't give a fuck what his 'badness' was supposed to be. I liked the guy.

And then one day he just disappeared. Well, it happens. But he is there in my gallery. Working the shadows.

I knew a girl who was my student. 30-something, nothing to sneeze at, and we would meet in a cafe. Then one day, I decided it would be better to meet in her apartment. At this suggestion, she mumbled and muttered, until I asked her what the problem was. More dissembling and clearing her throat until she finally said, "Well, I use my apartment for my work, and you might find it strange."

If she thought she was putting me off, she was wrong. I fairly leapt from my chair, overwhelmed by curiosity. "Why strange?"

She smiled an enigmatic Mona Lisa smile, as if deciding whether to…

"I am a dominatrix," she said. "That is my work."

Okay, I said, so let's have our next lesson at your apartment.

When we got there, a place high up in a building in some forgotten area of Moscow amid the expected shabby outer dimensions, I saw the machines she used to bastion her men down. Once they were in tow, she would "strap-on" a dildo and go to work on them. The size and color of the dildo was their choice. They had a great number to choose from: white and black, fat and thin. And BIG. Some, especially (of course) the black ones, were enormous.

"Who wants this?" I timidly asked.

"Mostly rich guys, even oligarchs." (Was she exaggerating?). "These guys always control and dominate and abuse other people," she explained. "But there is a side of them that wants the same as they give. They want to be beaten down and humiliated. It gets them off." Okay.

One day I arrived for our lesson, and Tanya was in a tizzy. A pipe had broken, and water was pouring out everywhere. She had called the superintendent but had not anticipated that he would come as soon as he said. Fifteen minutes. And she did not want this guy to know her profession.

"For Chrissakes, HELP me!!!" she cried ("Ради всего святого, помоги мне !!"), and so I was enlisted in the task of cramming dildos into as many open drawers as she could muster. In case you are wondering, it was really strange to be doing this - seizing plastic penises from their proud peacock shelves and stuffing them into hiding places under the innocent, Telkom powdered linen. But I guess I was a good sport. And by the time the plumber arrived, sheets had been thrown over those bulky contraptions which before you might have mistaken for dentist's chairs, and there was not a sculpted schlong to be found. It could have been modern art sequestered under those ballooning veils. The guy went to work, didn't bat an eye, and before long the tide was stemmed. He left and all the original interior decorating was restored as the English lesson proceeded. Evidently, she was expecting a visitor after we finished.

To see Tanya in broad daylight along the street or in a park would be to observe a perfectly normal-looking young woman. No vampirish glare, no ghoulish lip implants or lush purple lipstick. No stilettos to prod your groin with. Rather, a fitness club girl on whose feet roller blades would have fit nicely on a

Sunday afternoon. She dabbled in other professions: real estate, mood-enhancing herbal medicine, etc. But these ambitions would change with the weather. She was a meditative type with a sharp eye for money. Her face had a sensuous plainness that did not jump off the page at you but which, with its Russian hardness, somehow sent a blank, but desire-generating message.

It also happened that Tanya had a husband. How did she keep such a remarkable double life a secret from her unsuspecting spouse, you might wonder? In fact, he knew all about it. I have no idea what the terms of their 'prenup' might have been. Probably (this was Russia) nothing of the sort would have entered their minds.

He was not a pimp. Apparently, he earned his daily bread designing labels for cereal products. Or was it children's toys? It seems that he was occasionally even at home, relaxing in the bedroom, during the hours of action. I tried to imagine him back there, placidly watching Animal Planet or The Cooking Channel while, out in the dungeon, his wife was laying siege to some gasping - but ecstatic - Central Director. He had three choices - the husband, I mean: Cry "Stop!" Cry "Let me watch (or join in)!" Or stare at Animal Planet. Which evidently was what he opted for.

Tanya would have been unfazed either way. She had a conspiratorial way about her, a mischief-making mechanism in her dancing eyes as she prepared to enter - merrily, I imagined - into some 'squalid act of degradation'' that would have left the Keepers of the Faith dropping their jaws in scandalized yet mesmerized gasps of salivating disapproval.

One evening I went there and found her doing cocaine with another woman. I was invited into the circle. I guess I helped the girls make each other happy. Afterwards, Tanya hinted something about needing rent money, so I threw something on the table and left, my tongue soaked with their delicious mouths and vaginas and feet. The husband never appeared. Animal Planet must have been cracking that night.

The flesh is weak before the saintlike vow unless you prefer, truly prefer, martyrdom to the Maypole. Meanwhile, fetishes abound like strange birds on Pacific islands where there are no people at all.

So yes, that was the evening Tanya realized how much I love licking women's bare feet. So, the truth out, our lessons were different after that.

Anyway, it was cold that evening, and by the onset of the dark I was back in Preobrazhenska Plowshad. When I left the metro, fighting through all the people handing out flyers and wanting cigarettes or a drink, I saw another sight I still remember. A young woman was standing on the small embankment in front of the shops, and she was playing a violin.

Playing it well. She was tall and beautiful in that fiercely noble, impassive Russian way that has kept me in this country longer than I would ever have guessed. The spheres of her eyes seemed to have some sort of relationship with infinity, perhaps seeing everything, perhaps looking at nothing. Her fingers must have been awfully cold in the howling wind, but she wove the fiddle bow immaculately.
I threw some coins into her basket and waited to see if her marble eyes would make contact with me.

But they never did. She just kept playing.

FAREWELL TO THE VILLAGE

Контент 14+ (упоминание спаривания животных без описания процесса)

Translation: Content 14+ (mention of mating animals without describing the process)

Sitting on my balcony at sundown in Bliznatsi, Bulgaria, I prepare my mind to return to Moscow. It is hard to pull away this time, and one day I won't. I'll stay here. But for now, duty... and money... summon me back. Once upon a time, the very name 'Moscow" was a word containing what I will call "gray magic.' Intrigue, danger, seduction, inscrutability. Now it is just the mammoth city where I live and work. I think I have many friends in Moscow. I say, I think I do. My normally affirming spirit vacillates here because the concept of friendship is different now than it used to be. Now, like everything else, it moves too fast to seem real.

In Bliznatsi, nothing moves very fast at all. Early in the morning I take Casper and Poppy and we collect Bobby, our neighbor's alabaster pit bull, and we begin the long walk down the thistle-crowded path to the crescent of the valley leading to the forest and the sea. In some ways it was prettier in May before the harsh onslaught of the summer sun that brings temperatures of upwards 35 C, scalding and bleaching the fields. The heat kicks in at 8.00, but we begin our trek not much later than 7.00 and the undissolved mist is there to meet us, like a kind of fading night traffic that leaves only the dew to soak my trainers and feet. Usually this early there is no one about except, on the odd morning, a stout young athletic blonde who goes running with her dog. She is all business. There is also a guy who rides his moped to work, churning down the dusty path. I draw the animals aside, and he waves cheerfully at us as he glides past.

Sometimes the loggers come with their trucks, heading deep into the forest. Buying wood is a big deal here, because people need it for the long winter, and summer is the time to stock up. Of course, there is a lot of haggling over prices. The foreigners always think they are getting cheated by the wily locals. The gypsies also sell wood. We are advised to avoid them, and I have heard many "gypsy" stories. From this you would think they were the Devil's own special children, but something in me doubts this. After all, they are people, just like the rest of us and maybe, in the role of perpetual scapegoats, they help everyone else to feel better. But they are strange, and even the little girls' eye glitter like something from a Steven King novel. I like them.

The people here are either naturally dark, Bulgarian dark, or burnished to mahogany by the blistering sun. At the little supermarket a five minute walk away from my home, there is always a crowd. Some old toothless guys drink beer out front and nobody bothers them. You get the feeling that everybody knows everybody here, Everywhere on the outskirts of Bliznatsi there is construction, and I fear that one day soon the sense of "village" will be replaced by the reality of "town." Well, people are always building. You know how it is.

If morning here comes amid the gossip of birds and the trumpeting of roosters, the late morning reminds me of what Vivaldi must have felt when he composed the summer part of The Four Seasons. There is an electric vibrancy that sizzles in the air. The beach nearby - on the other side of the forest (but there are many beaches in the Varna area) - is packed with holiday-makers from Russia, Ukraine, Belarus, and elsewhere, including Bulgarians probably from inland cities like Plovdiv and Sofia. It is the mating season for them too. One sees the golden bodies of youth throbbing in their sensual moment. As Vivaldi shows us, the summer passion of southern countries is eternally electric.

Towards evening, the hot violins of the day give way to twilight breezes which start to sound like the strumming of a guitar, the mood slowly shifting to a minor key. It is now Sunday evening, and I rest on the balcony drinking in the wine of the wind - for me, even though it is only July, the last of the summer refreshment. I won't feel this in Moscow. I think it is because, even in the many splendid parks, the intimate communion between people and the landscape, the worm-rich loam of the earth, is lost. I watch. The old goat-swain - a man from the ancient world - leads his flock away to a distant mountain. It is like he is conducting an orchestra, using his staff like a wand to conjure a special language that twirls into the goat brains They baaa and bow. I talk to dogs that way. On the other side of the great undulation, three young guys on dirt-bikes send the dust a-flying, the faint purr of the engines lingering like a motor-driven lullaby. Across the field, the wiry men of the sun have spent the afternoon with combine harvesters, and much of the wild aspect of the panorama has received its perfunctory summer haircut. The resulting hay is scattered now in bales secured by wire. The word "harvest" enters my mind. A good word, suggesting the human being and the land, such an ancient coalition, and the setting sun is the same sun that Cleopatra and Marc Antony saw. The same sun that those in the Bronze Age saw. And before.

Our evening walk. And now a few black storm clouds gather, sending shivers through the trees. The earth is vast and silent except for the chords in the dark olive gown of the forest, guitar passages now changing into the thunder of stark, almost menacing Rachmaninoff piano keys. Hearing such growling from above, the dogs glance at me apprehensively. I want to say, "Guys, why look at me?" But we continue our way, and soon the heavy black-water clouds have disappeared and argue no more. Rejuvenated, the dogs dart into the remaining tickets at the bas e of the forest, chasing some rabbit or doggy dream of heaven knows what. Overhead, I watch the birds of evening as they glide and swoop, pelicans and shrikes observing the fields with a wild surmise that knows everything. Everything that I don't know, they know. The forest is deep and powerful, and the onset of darkness out here humbles the soul and troubles the nerves. At night, ghosts wake up from inside the trees and wander in the dark. That is why the forest dogs give up their plaintive howls.

And now, amid this darkening greenery of isolation, death, and rebirth, I glance skyward and see an airplane - a commercial airliner bound for Turkey or Russia or some other equally imaginary destination, silently navigating the sky. I know that people are inside that capsule having their small dinners, reading, snoozing. I confess to fear of flying, but they seem utterly safe up there, well-protected and at peace. There is no technology involved, it appears. They are merely ancient mariners sailing away to another place, in no hurry at all as their slender, sturdy boat parts the heavens and rides to sanctuary on the sea-waves of the nocturnal skies.

About the Author

Eric Le Roy was born in Morgantown, West Virginia. After earning a Ph.D. in Creative Writing at Florida State University, he published numerous poems and stories and began a new career as an English as Second Language tutor, which has enabled him to live in multiple locations around the world, including a ten-year stint in Russia. He now resides in a Bulgarian village with his wife Liubov, two beloved dogs, and a much-revered cat.

Made in the USA
Middletown, DE
25 June 2021